Overview

"Becoming a YouTube Sensation: the 30-Day Guide" is a comprehensive book that provides a step-by-step roadmap for aspiring YouTube creators to achieve viral success in just 30 days. This book covers everything from understanding the YouTube platform and setting goals, to creating compelling content, building an audience, optimizing your channel, monetizing your videos, engaging with your audience, promoting your videos, collaborating with other YouTubers, overcoming challenges, expanding your YouTube presence, and measuring success. With practical tips, strategies, and insights, this guide is a must-have for anyone looking to make their mark in the world of YouTube." Chapter 1: "Introduction to YouTube Sensation" introduces readers to the YouTube platform and helps them understand its potential for success. It guides them in setting goals and identifying their niche, as well as creating a compelling channel brand that stands out from the crowd. Chapter 2: "Content Creation Strategies" dives into the art of creating engaging videos. It provides tips on developing video ideas, scripting and storyboarding, shooting and editing techniques, and optimizing video quality and length to keep viewers hooked. Chapter 3: "Building an Audience" focuses on understanding the target audience and promoting the channel on social media. It also explores the power of collaborations with other YouTubers, engaging with viewers, utilizing SEO for discoverability, and analyzing YouTube analytics for growth.

Table Of Contents

1 Introduction to YouTube Sensation

1.1 Understanding the YouTube Platform

YouTube has become one of the most popular platforms for content creators to showcase their talent, share their knowledge, and connect with a global audience. With over 2 billion monthly active users, YouTube offers immense opportunities for individuals to become YouTube sensations and build a successful career online. However, to achieve this level of success, it is crucial to understand the YouTube platform and how it works.

1.1.1 The Power of YouTube

YouTube is not just a video-sharing platform; it is a social media giant that has revolutionized the way we consume and share video content. It allows users to upload, view, and interact with videos on a wide range of topics. From educational tutorials to entertaining skits, YouTube offers something for everyone.

One of the key reasons why YouTube has become so popular is its accessibility. Anyone with an internet connection and a camera can create and upload videos to the platform. This democratization of content creation has given rise to a diverse community of creators who cater to various niches and interests.

1.1.2 YouTube's Algorithm

To understand how to become a YouTube sensation, it is essential to grasp the concept of YouTube's algorithm. The algorithm determines which videos are recommended to users based on various factors such as watch time, engagement, and relevance. By understanding how the algorithm works, you can optimize your content to increase its visibility and reach a wider audience.

YouTube's algorithm takes into account several key metrics, including:

1. Watch Time: The total amount of time viewers spend watching your videos.
2. Engagement: The number of likes, comments, shares, and subscribers your videos receive.
3. Click-Through Rate (CTR): The percentage of viewers who click on your video after seeing it in search results or recommendations.
4. Viewer Retention: How long viewers watch your videos before clicking away or closing the tab.
5. Relevance: How well your video matches the viewer's search query or interests.

By focusing on these metrics and creating high-quality, engaging content, you can increase your chances of appearing in YouTube's search results and recommendations, ultimately attracting more viewers to your channel.

1.1.3 YouTube's Community Guidelines and Policies

As a YouTube creator, it is crucial to familiarize yourself with YouTube's community guidelines and policies. These guidelines outline the types of content that are allowed on the platform and the actions that can result in penalties or account termination.

Some key points to keep in mind include:

1. Copyright Infringement: Avoid using copyrighted material without permission or proper attribution.
2. Hate Speech and Harassment: Do not engage in or promote hate speech, harassment, or bullying.
3. Nudity and Sexual Content: YouTube has strict policies regarding explicit or adult content.
4. Misleading Content: Do not create or promote misleading or deceptive content.
5. Advertiser-Friendly Content: Ensure that your content is suitable for advertisers to maintain monetization opportunities.

By adhering to these guidelines and policies, you can create a safe and welcoming environment for your viewers and avoid any potential penalties or restrictions on your channel.

1.1.4 YouTube's Monetization and Partner Program

YouTube offers creators the opportunity to monetize their content through the YouTube Partner Program. This program allows eligible creators to earn money from advertisements displayed on their videos. To qualify for the program, you need to meet certain criteria, including a minimum number of subscribers and watch hours.

Monetizing your channel can provide a significant source of income, but it is important to note that it is not the only way to make money on YouTube. There are various alternative revenue streams, such as brand partnerships, merchandise sales, and crowdfunding, which can supplement your earnings and diversify your income sources.

Understanding the YouTube platform is the first step towards becoming a YouTube sensation. By familiarizing yourself with YouTube's algorithm, community guidelines, and monetization opportunities, you can lay a solid foundation for your journey to success. In the following chapters, we will delve deeper into setting goals, identifying your niche, and creating a compelling channel brand to help you become a viral YouTube video creator in 30 days or less.

1.2 Setting Goals for YouTube Success

Setting clear and achievable goals is crucial for your journey to becoming a YouTube sensation. Without goals, it can be challenging to stay focused and motivated. In this section, we will discuss the importance of setting goals and provide you with a step-by-step guide on how to set effective goals for your YouTube channel.

Why Setting Goals is Important

Setting goals is essential because it gives you direction and purpose. It helps you define what you want to achieve and provides a roadmap to get there. Without goals, you may find yourself aimlessly creating content without a clear vision of where you want to go.

Here are a few reasons why setting goals is crucial for YouTube success:

1. **Motivation:** Goals provide you with a sense of purpose and motivation. When you have a clear target in mind, you are more likely to stay committed and dedicated to your channel.
2. **Focus:** Setting goals helps you prioritize your efforts and focus on what matters most. It allows you to allocate your time and resources effectively, ensuring that you are working towards your desired outcomes.
3. **Measurable Progress:** Goals provide a benchmark for measuring your progress. By setting specific and measurable goals, you can track your achievements and make adjustments along the way.
4. **Accountability:** When you set goals, you hold yourself accountable for your success. It helps you stay disciplined and committed to the tasks necessary to achieve your objectives.

Step-by-Step Guide to Setting Goals

Now that you understand the importance of setting goals, let's dive into a step-by-step guide to help you set effective goals for your YouTube channel:

1. Identify Your Long-Term Vision

Start by envisioning where you want your YouTube channel to be in the long run. What is your ultimate goal? Do you want to become a full-time YouTuber, reach a specific number of subscribers, or generate a certain income? Clearly define your long-term vision to guide your goal-setting process.

2. Break It Down into Short-Term Goals

Once you have a clear long-term vision, break it down into smaller, achievable short-term goals. These goals should be specific, measurable, attainable, relevant, and time-bound (SMART goals). For example, if your long-term vision is to reach 100,000 subscribers, a short-term goal could be to gain 1,000 subscribers in the next month.

3. Prioritize Your Goals

Not all goals are created equal. Prioritize your goals based on their importance and impact on your channel's growth. Focus on goals that will have the most significant impact and align with your long-term vision. This will help you stay focused and avoid spreading yourself too thin.

4. Set Actionable Steps

Once you have identified your short-term goals, break them down into actionable steps. These steps should outline the specific tasks you need to complete to achieve each goal. For example, if your goal is to improve video quality, actionable steps could include investing in better equipment, learning editing techniques, and practicing storytelling.

5. Set Deadlines

Assign deadlines to each goal and actionable step. Deadlines create a sense of urgency and help you stay on track. Be realistic with your deadlines, considering the time and resources available to you. Setting deadlines will also allow you to measure your progress and make adjustments if necessary.

6. Review and Adjust

Regularly review your goals and assess your progress. Are you on track? Are there any obstacles or challenges that need to be addressed? Be flexible and willing to adjust your goals if needed. As you gain more experience and insights, your goals may evolve, and that's perfectly normal.

7. Celebrate Milestones

When you achieve a goal or reach a milestone, take the time to celebrate your accomplishments. Celebrating your successes will boost your motivation and reinforce your commitment to your YouTube journey. It's essential to acknowledge and appreciate the progress you have made.

Conclusion

Setting goals is a fundamental step in your path to YouTube success. It provides you with direction, motivation, and a roadmap to achieve your desired outcomes. By following the step-by-step guide outlined in this section, you can set effective goals for your YouTube channel and stay focused on your journey to becoming a YouTube sensation. Remember, setting goals is just the beginning; it's your dedication, consistency, and passion that will ultimately lead you to success.

1.3 Identifying Your Niche

In order to become a successful YouTube sensation, it is crucial to identify your niche. Your niche is the specific topic or theme that your channel will revolve around. Choosing the right niche is essential for several reasons. Firstly, it helps you establish yourself as an expert in a particular area, which can attract a loyal and engaged audience. Secondly, it allows you to create content that you are passionate about, which will make the process more enjoyable for you. Lastly, having a niche makes it easier for viewers to find your channel and understand what type of content they can expect from you.

1.3.1 Assess Your Interests and Expertise

The first step in identifying your niche is to assess your interests and expertise. Think about the topics that you are genuinely passionate about and knowledgeable in. Consider your hobbies, skills, and areas of expertise. It is important to choose a niche that you genuinely enjoy and have a deep understanding of, as this will make it easier for you to create high-quality content consistently.

1.3.2 Research Popular and Trending Topics

Once you have identified your interests and expertise, it is essential to research popular and trending topics within those areas. This will help you understand what type of content is in demand and what topics are currently popular among viewers. Use YouTube's search bar and explore related channels to get an idea of what topics are gaining traction. Additionally, you can use keyword research tools to identify popular search terms related to your niche.

1.3.3 Narrow Down Your Niche

After conducting research, it is time to narrow down your niche. While it may be tempting to cover a broad range of topics to attract a larger audience, it is generally more effective to focus on a specific niche. This allows you to establish yourself as an authority in that area and attract a dedicated audience.

For example, instead of creating a general fitness channel, you could focus on a specific niche like yoga for beginners or high-intensity interval training (HIIT) workouts.

1.3.4 Consider Your Target Audience

When identifying your niche, it is crucial to consider your target audience. Think about who your ideal viewers are and what type of content they would be interested in. Consider their demographics, interests, and preferences. Understanding your target audience will help you tailor your content to their needs and preferences, increasing the chances of attracting and retaining viewers.

1.3.5 Differentiate Yourself

In a saturated platform like YouTube, it is important to differentiate yourself from the competition. Once you have identified your niche, think about how you can bring a unique perspective or approach to the topic. Consider what sets you apart from other creators in your niche and how you can add value to your viewers' experience. This could be through your personality, storytelling style, or the format of your videos.

1.3.6 Test and Refine

Identifying your niche is not a one-time decision. It is an ongoing process that requires testing and refinement. Once you have chosen your niche, start creating content and pay attention to the response from your audience. Analyze your video metrics, read comments, and engage with your viewers to understand what type of content resonates with them the most. Use this feedback to refine your niche and make adjustments to your content strategy if necessary.

1.3.7 Stay Flexible

While it is important to have a niche, it is also crucial to stay flexible and adapt to changes in the YouTube landscape. Trends and viewer preferences can change rapidly, so it is important to stay up-to-date with the latest developments in your niche and be willing to pivot if necessary. This could involve exploring new topics within your niche or even expanding into related niches that align with your interests and expertise.

1.3.8 Be Authentic

Lastly, when identifying your niche, it is essential to be authentic. Choose a niche that aligns with your values and passions. Authenticity is key to building a genuine connection with your audience and establishing trust. Viewers can sense when someone is not being genuine, so it is important to choose a niche that you are truly passionate about and can speak about with authenticity and authority.

By following these steps, you will be able to identify your niche and set the foundation for a successful YouTube channel. Remember, choosing the right niche is crucial for attracting and retaining viewers, so take the time to assess your interests, research popular topics, and consider your target audience. Stay flexible, be authentic, and most importantly, have fun creating content in your chosen niche.

1.4 Creating a Compelling Channel Brand

Creating a compelling channel brand is essential for standing out in the crowded world of YouTube. Your channel brand is what sets you apart from other creators and helps viewers identify and connect with your content. In this section, we will explore the key elements of creating a compelling channel brand that will attract and engage your target audience.

1.4.1 Defining Your Channel's Identity

Before you can create a compelling channel brand, you need to define your channel's identity. Start by asking yourself the following questions:

1. What is the main focus of your channel? Are you a beauty guru, a gaming enthusiast, or a travel vlogger? Identifying your niche will help you target a specific audience and create content that resonates with them.
2. What is your unique selling point? What makes your channel different from others in your niche? It could be your personality, your expertise, or your storytelling skills. Highlighting your unique qualities will help you stand out and attract viewers.
3. Who is your target audience? Understanding your target audience is crucial for creating content that appeals to them. Consider their demographics, interests, and preferences. This will guide your content creation and branding decisions.

Once you have a clear understanding of your channel's identity, you can move on to creating a compelling channel brand.

1.4.2 Channel Name and Logo

Your channel name and logo are the first things viewers see when they come across your content. They should be memorable, reflective of your channel's identity, and visually appealing. Here are some tips for creating an effective channel name and logo:

1. Channel Name:
   - o Keep it short and easy to remember.
   - o Make it relevant to your niche or content.
   - o Avoid using numbers or special characters that can make it difficult to search for your channel.
   - o Consider using your own name if you are the face of your channel.
2. Logo:
   - o Design a logo that represents your channel's identity and niche.
   - o Use colors and fonts that align with your brand's personality.
   - o Ensure that your logo is scalable and looks good across different devices and platforms.
   - o Consider hiring a professional designer if you don't have design skills.

Remember, your channel name and logo should be consistent with your overall brand identity and help viewers recognize your content.

1.4.3 Channel Art and Thumbnails

Channel art and thumbnails play a crucial role in attracting viewers and enticing them to click on your videos. Here are some tips for creating compelling channel art and thumbnails:

1. Channel Art:
   - o Use high-resolution images that represent your channel's niche or content.
   - o Include your channel name or logo in the channel art.
   - o Keep the design clean and uncluttered.
   - o Consider updating your channel art periodically to keep it fresh and relevant.

2. Thumbnails:
   o Create eye-catching thumbnails that grab viewers' attention.
   o Use high-quality images or screenshots from your videos.
   o Include text or graphics that convey the main idea or benefit of watching the video.
   o Maintain consistency in thumbnail design to establish a recognizable brand.

Both channel art and thumbnails should be visually appealing, consistent with your brand identity, and accurately represent the content of your videos.

1.4.4 Channel Trailer

A channel trailer is a short video that introduces new viewers to your channel and gives them a taste of what they can expect from your content. It is an excellent opportunity to showcase your personality, highlight your best videos, and engage viewers. Here are some tips for creating an effective channel trailer:

1. Keep it short and engaging. Aim for a duration of 1-2 minutes.
2. Introduce yourself and explain what your channel is about.
3. Show snippets of your best videos to give viewers a sense of your content.
4. Include a call-to-action at the end, encouraging viewers to subscribe or watch more videos.
5. Use high-quality footage and editing techniques to make your trailer visually appealing.

Your channel trailer should leave a lasting impression on viewers and make them want to explore more of your content.

1.4.5 Consistent Branding Across Platforms

To create a strong and recognizable channel brand, it is essential to maintain consistent branding across different platforms. This includes your YouTube channel, social media profiles, website (if applicable), and any other online presence. Here are some tips for consistent branding:

1. Use the same channel name, logo, and channel art across all platforms.
2. Maintain a consistent tone and style in your content and captions.
3. Use similar color schemes, fonts, and visual elements in your branding materials.
4. Cross-promote your content across platforms to increase visibility and engagement.

Consistent branding helps viewers recognize your content wherever they encounter it and builds trust and loyalty with your audience.

1.4.6 Engaging Channel Description

Your channel description is an opportunity to introduce yourself, explain your content, and engage viewers. It should be concise, informative, and compelling. Here are some tips for writing an engaging channel description:

1. Start with a catchy and attention-grabbing opening sentence.
2. Clearly explain what your channel is about and what viewers can expect.
3. Highlight your unique selling points and what sets you apart from other creators.
4. Include links to your social media profiles or website to encourage further engagement.
5. Use keywords relevant to your niche to improve discoverability in search results.

Remember to update your channel description periodically to reflect any changes in your content or branding.

Creating a compelling channel brand takes time and effort, but it is a crucial step towards becoming a YouTube sensation. By defining your channel's identity, creating visually appealing branding materials, and maintaining consistency across platforms, you will attract and engage your target audience, setting the stage for long-term success.

2 Content Creation Strategies

2.1 Developing Engaging Video Ideas

One of the most crucial aspects of becoming a YouTube sensation is developing engaging video ideas. Your content is the heart and soul of your channel, and it is what will attract and retain viewers. In this section, we will explore various strategies and techniques to help you generate creative and captivating video ideas that will resonate with your target audience.

2.1.1 Understanding Your Target Audience

Before you start brainstorming video ideas, it is essential to have a clear understanding of your target audience. Who are they? What are their interests, preferences, and needs? Conducting thorough research and creating audience personas can provide valuable insights into the type of content that will resonate with your viewers.

Consider demographics such as age, gender, location, and interests. Additionally, analyze the comments and feedback from your existing viewers to gain a deeper understanding of their preferences. This information will serve as a foundation for developing video ideas that cater to your audience's specific needs and desires.

2.1.2 Identifying Trends and Topics

Staying up-to-date with the latest trends and topics within your niche is crucial for developing engaging video ideas. Monitor popular YouTube channels, social media platforms, news outlets, and industry blogs to identify emerging trends and topics that are generating buzz.

By incorporating trending topics into your content, you increase the likelihood of attracting a wider audience and gaining more exposure. However, it is important to strike a balance between following trends and staying true to your channel's unique style and niche. Authenticity is key to building a loyal and engaged audience.

2.1.3 Brainstorming Sessions

Brainstorming sessions are an effective way to generate a wide range of video ideas. Set aside dedicated time to brainstorm and let your creativity flow. Here are a few techniques to help you during your brainstorming sessions:

1. Mind Mapping: Start with a central theme or topic and branch out with related ideas. This visual representation can help you explore different angles and perspectives.
2. Word Association: Write down a word or phrase related to your niche and then brainstorm related words or ideas. This technique can help you uncover unique and unexpected video ideas.
3. Problem-Solution Approach: Identify common problems or challenges faced by your target audience and brainstorm video ideas that provide solutions or valuable insights.
4. Collaborative Brainstorming: Invite friends, fellow YouTubers, or members of your target audience to participate in a brainstorming session. Different perspectives can lead to innovative and engaging video ideas.

2.1.4 Analyzing Competitors

Analyzing your competitors' content can provide inspiration and insights into what works well within your niche. Take note of the type of videos that are performing exceptionally well, the format they use, and the engagement they receive from viewers.

However, it is crucial to avoid copying or imitating your competitors' content directly. Instead, use their success as a source of inspiration to create unique and original video ideas that align with your brand and style.

2.1.5 Engaging Storytelling

Storytelling is a powerful tool for creating engaging and memorable videos. Incorporate storytelling techniques into your content to captivate your audience and keep them hooked from start to finish. Whether it's sharing personal experiences, anecdotes, or narratives related to your niche, storytelling adds depth and emotional connection to your videos.

Consider the structure of your videos, including a compelling introduction, a well-paced narrative, and a satisfying conclusion. This will help create a cohesive and engaging storytelling experience for your viewers.

2.1.6 Audience Interaction and Feedback

Engaging with your audience and seeking their input can be an excellent source of video ideas. Encourage your viewers to leave comments, suggestions, and feedback on your videos or social media platforms. Pay attention to the questions they ask, the topics they are interested in, and the challenges they face. This direct interaction with your audience can provide valuable insights and inspiration for future video ideas.

Additionally, consider conducting polls, surveys, or Q&A sessions to actively involve your audience in the content creation process. This not only helps generate video ideas but also strengthens the bond between you and your viewers.

2.1.7 Experimentation and Innovation

Don't be afraid to step out of your comfort zone and experiment with different video formats, styles, and topics. Innovation and creativity are key to standing out in the crowded YouTube landscape. Test new ideas, explore different niches, and push the boundaries of your content to keep your audience engaged and excited.

Remember, developing engaging video ideas is an ongoing process. Continuously monitor the performance of your videos, listen to your audience's feedback, and adapt your content strategy accordingly. By staying open to new ideas and consistently delivering high-quality content, you will increase your chances of becoming a YouTube sensation.

2.2 Scripting and Storyboarding Your Videos

Creating engaging and compelling content is crucial to becoming a YouTube sensation. While spontaneity can be effective in some cases, having a well-thought-out script and storyboard can greatly enhance the quality and impact of your videos. In this section, we will explore the importance of scripting and storyboarding and provide you with a step-by-step guide on how to effectively plan your videos.

Why Scripting and Storyboarding Matter

Scripting and storyboarding are essential steps in the video creation process as they help you organize your thoughts, structure your content, and ensure a smooth flow of information. Here are a few reasons why scripting and storyboarding matter:

1. **Clarity and Coherence**: By scripting your videos, you can articulate your ideas clearly and concisely. This helps you avoid rambling or going off-topic, ensuring that your viewers understand your message.
2. **Time Efficiency**: Having a script allows you to plan your content in advance, saving you time during the recording and editing process. It helps you stay focused and reduces the need for multiple takes.
3. **Engagement**: A well-scripted video is more likely to captivate your audience and keep them engaged throughout. It allows you to deliver your message effectively, making your content more memorable and shareable.
4. **Professionalism**: Scripting and storyboarding demonstrate a level of professionalism and preparation that can set you apart from other creators. It shows that you value your viewers' time and are committed to delivering high-quality content.

Step-by-Step Guide to Scripting and Storyboarding

Now that we understand the importance of scripting and storyboarding, let's dive into the step-by-step process of creating a script and storyboard for your videos:

Step 1: Define Your Objective

Before you start scripting, it's essential to define the objective of your video. Ask yourself what you want to achieve with this particular video. Are you trying to educate, entertain, inspire, or inform your audience? Having a clear objective will guide your script and ensure that your content aligns with your goals.

Step 2: Research and Gather Information

Once you have a clear objective, conduct thorough research on the topic of your video. Gather relevant information, statistics, examples, and anecdotes that support your message. This will help you provide valuable and accurate content to your viewers.

Step 3: Outline Your Script

Create an outline for your script, breaking it down into sections or key points. This will serve as a roadmap for your video and help you maintain a logical flow. Start with an attention-grabbing introduction, followed by the main body of your content, and conclude with a strong call-to-action or summary.

Step 4: Write Your Script

Using your outline as a guide, start writing your script. Keep your language conversational and engaging, ensuring that it resonates with your target audience. Use bullet points or short sentences to make it easier to read and follow during recording.

Step 5: Practice and Refine

Once you have written your script, practice reading it aloud several times. Pay attention to your tone, pacing, and pronunciation. Refine your script as needed, making it sound natural and authentic. Consider adding pauses or emphasis to enhance the delivery of key points.

Step 6: Create a Storyboard

A storyboard is a visual representation of your video, consisting of a series of sketches or images that depict each scene or shot. It helps you visualize the flow of your video and plan your shots accordingly. You can use simple drawings, stick figures, or even screenshots from similar videos as placeholders.

Step 7: Plan Your Shots and Visuals

Based on your script and storyboard, plan the shots and visuals you want to include in your video. Consider the camera angles, transitions, and any additional elements such as graphics or text overlays. This will help you create a visually appealing and engaging video.

Step 8: Review and Revise

Before you start recording, review your script and storyboard one final time. Make any necessary revisions or adjustments to ensure that everything is in order. This will save you time and minimize errors during the recording and editing process.

Conclusion

Scripting and storyboarding are essential steps in creating high-quality and engaging YouTube videos. By following the step-by-step guide provided in this section, you can effectively plan your content, deliver your message with clarity, and captivate your audience. Remember, preparation is key to success, and investing time in scripting and storyboarding will greatly contribute to your journey of becoming a YouTube sensation.

2.3 Shooting and Editing Techniques

Once you have developed engaging video ideas and scripted your content, it's time to focus on shooting and editing techniques to bring your vision to life. The quality of your videos plays a crucial role in attracting and retaining viewers, so it's important to pay attention to the details. In this section, we will explore some essential shooting and editing techniques that will help you create professional-looking videos that stand out on YouTube.

2.3.1 Equipment and Setup

Before you start shooting your videos, it's important to have the right equipment and setup. While you don't need to invest in expensive gear right away, having a few essential items can significantly improve the quality of your videos. Here are some equipment recommendations:

1. Camera: While smartphones can capture decent video quality, consider investing in a dedicated camera for better results. Look for a camera that offers high-resolution video recording and has good low-light performance.
2. Tripod or Stabilizer: To avoid shaky footage, use a tripod or stabilizer to keep your camera steady. This will help maintain a professional and polished look.
3. Lighting: Good lighting is essential for creating visually appealing videos. Natural light is ideal, so try to shoot near a window or in a well-lit room. If necessary, invest in affordable lighting kits to ensure consistent and well-lit videos.
4. Microphone: Clear audio is just as important as good video quality. Invest in a decent external microphone to capture high-quality sound and reduce background noise.

Once you have your equipment ready, set up your shooting space. Make sure the background is clean and clutter-free, and consider adding some props or decorations that align with your channel's branding. Test the lighting and audio setup before you start shooting to ensure everything is working properly.

2.3.2 Framing and Composition

When shooting your videos, pay attention to framing and composition to create visually appealing content. Here are some tips to keep in mind:

1. Rule of Thirds: Imagine dividing your frame into a grid of nine equal parts using two horizontal and two vertical lines. Position your subject along these lines or at the intersections to create a balanced and visually pleasing composition.
2. Headroom and Lead Room: Leave some space above your subject's head (headroom) and in front of them (lead room) to create a natural and aesthetically pleasing composition.
3. Depth and Perspective: Create depth in your shots by including elements in the foreground, middle ground, and background. This adds visual interest and makes your videos more engaging.
4. Rule of Space: When shooting a moving subject, leave some space in the frame in the direction they are moving. This creates a sense of movement and adds dynamism to your videos.

Experiment with different angles and perspectives to find what works best for your content. Don't be afraid to try unconventional shots to add variety and creativity to your videos.

2.3.3 Shooting Techniques

Now that you have your equipment set up and understand the basics of framing and composition, let's explore some shooting techniques to enhance the quality of your videos:

1. Manual Focus: If your camera allows it, consider using manual focus instead of relying on autofocus. This gives you more control over what you want to focus on and ensures sharp and crisp footage.

2. B-roll Footage: B-roll refers to additional footage that complements your main shots. Incorporating B-roll adds visual interest and helps you tell a more compelling story. Capture footage of relevant details, close-ups, or behind-the-scenes moments to enhance your videos.

3. Camera Movement: Experiment with camera movements such as panning (horizontal movement), tilting (vertical movement), and tracking (following a subject's movement). Smooth camera movements can add a professional touch to your videos.

4. White Balance: Adjust the white balance settings on your camera to ensure accurate colors in different lighting conditions. This will prevent your videos from looking too warm or too cool.

2.3.4 Editing Techniques

Once you have captured your footage, it's time to edit your videos to create a polished final product. Here are some editing techniques to consider:

1. Trim and Cut: Remove any unnecessary footage and trim your clips to keep your videos concise and engaging. Cut out any mistakes or awkward pauses to maintain a smooth flow.

2. Transitions: Use transitions to create seamless transitions between clips. Popular transitions include fade-ins, fade-outs, crossfades, and slide transitions. Experiment with different transitions to find what suits your content.

3. Color Correction: Adjust the colors and tones of your footage to create a consistent and visually appealing look. Use color correction tools to correct any color imbalances and enhance the overall aesthetic of your videos.

4. Audio Editing: Clean up your audio by removing background noise, adjusting volume levels, and adding music or sound effects. Ensure that your voice is clear and easily understandable.

5. Text and Graphics: Incorporate text overlays, lower thirds, and graphics to provide additional information or enhance the visual storytelling of your videos. Use text and graphics sparingly to avoid overwhelming your viewers.

6. Music and Sound Effects: Choose appropriate music and sound effects to enhance the mood and atmosphere of your videos. Ensure that the audio complements the visuals and doesn't overpower the narration or dialogue.

Remember to maintain a consistent style and branding throughout your videos. Use the same fonts, colors, and graphics to create a cohesive and recognizable channel identity.

Conclusion

Shooting and editing techniques are essential skills for creating high-quality videos that captivate your audience. By paying attention to equipment, framing, composition, shooting techniques, and editing techniques, you can elevate the production value of your videos and stand out on YouTube. Practice these techniques, experiment with different styles, and continuously strive to improve your skills. With time and dedication, you'll be able to create compelling and visually stunning content that resonates with your viewers.

2.4 Optimizing Video Quality and Length

When it comes to creating YouTube videos, two important factors that can greatly impact the success of your channel are video quality and length. In this section, we will explore strategies to optimize these aspects of your content to attract and retain viewers.

2.4.1 Enhancing Video Quality

The quality of your videos plays a crucial role in capturing the attention of your audience and keeping them engaged. Here are some tips to enhance the video quality of your content:

1. **Invest in good equipment**: While you don't need to break the bank, having decent equipment can significantly improve the overall quality of your videos. Consider investing in a good camera, microphone, and lighting setup to ensure clear visuals and crisp audio.

2. **Choose the right resolution**: YouTube supports various video resolutions, including 720p, 1080p, and even 4K. Selecting the appropriate resolution for your content is essential. Higher resolutions provide better clarity, but keep in mind that larger file sizes may affect upload and streaming speeds.

3. **Pay attention to lighting**: Proper lighting can make a significant difference in the quality of your videos. Ensure that your subject is well-lit, avoiding harsh shadows or overexposure. Natural light or softbox lighting can help create a professional look.

4. **Capture clear audio**: Poor audio quality can be a major turn-off for viewers. Invest in a good microphone or use an external audio recorder to capture clear and crisp sound. Consider using a windscreen or pop filter to reduce unwanted noise.

5. **Edit and enhance**: Post-production editing can greatly enhance the quality of your videos. Use video editing software to trim unnecessary

footage, adjust colors, add transitions, and incorporate other effects to make your content visually appealing.

2.4.2 Finding the Optimal Video Length

The length of your videos is another crucial aspect to consider. While there is no one-size-fits-all answer, finding the optimal video length for your content can help keep your viewers engaged and increase the likelihood of them watching your videos in their entirety. Here are some guidelines to consider:

1. **Know your audience**: Understanding your target audience is key to determining the ideal video length. Consider the preferences and attention spans of your viewers. For example, if your content is educational or instructional, shorter videos of 5-10 minutes may be more effective. However, if you are creating vlogs or entertainment-based content, longer videos of 15-20 minutes or more may be suitable.

2. **Focus on quality over quantity**: While it can be tempting to create longer videos to increase watch time, it's important to prioritize quality content. Ensure that your videos are engaging, informative, and provide value to your viewers. If you can deliver your message effectively in a shorter time frame, it's better to keep your videos concise.

3. **Experiment and analyze**: Pay attention to your video analytics to gain insights into viewer behavior. Analyze metrics such as average watch time, audience retention, and engagement to understand how your audience responds to different video lengths. Experiment with varying lengths and monitor the performance to identify trends and patterns.

4. **Consider video format**: The type of content you create can also influence the optimal video length. For example, tutorials or product reviews may require more time to provide detailed information, while comedic sketches or music videos may be more effective when kept shorter.

5. **Engage your audience**: Regardless of the video length, it's crucial to engage your audience from the beginning. Hook them with an attention-grabbing introduction and maintain their interest throughout the video. Use storytelling techniques, visuals, and a dynamic presentation style to keep viewers engaged.

Remember, the optimal video length may vary depending on your niche, target audience, and content type. It's important to continuously monitor and adapt your approach based on viewer feedback and analytics to find the sweet spot that works best for your channel.

By optimizing the quality of your videos and finding the right length, you can create content that captivates your audience, encourages them to watch more of your videos, and increases the chances of your content being shared and going viral.

3 Building an Audience

3.1 Understanding Your Target Audience

Before you can effectively build an audience on YouTube, it is crucial to have a deep understanding of your target audience. Your target audience consists of the people who are most likely to be interested in your content and become loyal viewers. By understanding their needs, preferences, and behaviors, you can create content that resonates with them and attracts their attention. In this section, we will explore various strategies to help you gain a better understanding of your target audience.

3.1.1 Conducting Market Research

To understand your target audience, you need to conduct thorough market research. This involves gathering information about your potential viewers, their demographics, interests, and online behaviors. Here are some steps to help you conduct effective market research:

1. Define your target audience: Start by clearly defining who your ideal viewers are. Consider factors such as age, gender, location, interests, and preferences. This will help you narrow down your focus and create content that appeals to a specific group of people.
2. Analyze competitor channels: Study the channels of your competitors or creators in a similar niche. Look at the type of content they create, the engagement they receive, and the demographics of their audience. This will give you insights into what works well in your niche and help you identify gaps that you can fill with your content.
3. Use analytics tools: YouTube provides analytics tools that can give you valuable information about your viewers. Use these tools to analyze the demographics of your existing audience, their viewing habits, and the performance of your videos. This data will help you identify patterns and make informed decisions about your content strategy.

4. Conduct surveys and interviews: Reach out to your existing viewers or potential viewers through surveys and interviews. Ask them about their preferences, what they enjoy about your content, and what they would like to see more of. This direct feedback will provide you with valuable insights into the needs and expectations of your target audience.

3.1.2 Creating Buyer Personas

Once you have gathered the necessary information about your target audience, it is helpful to create buyer personas. A buyer persona is a fictional representation of your ideal viewer, based on the data you have collected. It helps you visualize and understand your audience on a deeper level. Here are some steps to create effective buyer personas:

1. Identify common characteristics: Look for commonalities among your target audience. Identify their age range, gender, occupation, interests, and any other relevant characteristics. This will help you create a clear picture of who your ideal viewer is.
2. Give them a name and backstory: To make your buyer personas more relatable, give them a name and create a backstory. Think about their motivations, goals, and challenges. This will help you understand their needs and tailor your content to address those needs.
3. Understand their goals and pain points: Identify the goals and pain points of your buyer personas. What are they looking to achieve by watching your videos? What challenges do they face that your content can help them overcome? Understanding these aspects will enable you to create content that provides value and resonates with your audience.
4. Consider their preferred content format: Determine the preferred content format of your buyer personas. Do they prefer tutorials, vlogs, reviews, or something else? Knowing their preferred format will help you create content that aligns with their preferences and keeps them engaged.

3.1.3 Engaging with Your Audience

Once you have a clear understanding of your target audience, it is essential to engage with them regularly. Building a loyal audience requires ongoing interaction and communication. Here are some strategies to help you engage with your audience effectively:

1. Respond to comments: Take the time to respond to comments on your videos. Engage in conversations, answer questions, and show appreciation for your viewers' feedback. This will make your audience feel valued and encourage them to continue engaging with your content.
2. Encourage feedback and suggestions: Ask your viewers for feedback and suggestions on your content. This can be done through comments, polls, or dedicated feedback videos. By involving your audience in the content creation process, you make them feel like a part of your community and build a stronger connection.
3. Conduct live streams and Q&A sessions: Live streams and Q&A sessions provide an opportunity for real-time interaction with your audience. Use these sessions to answer questions, share insights, and get to know your viewers better. This direct interaction helps foster a sense of community and strengthens the bond between you and your audience.
4. Utilize social media platforms: Extend your engagement beyond YouTube by utilizing social media platforms. Interact with your audience on platforms such as Twitter, Instagram, and Facebook. Share behind-the-scenes content, updates, and engage in conversations. This multi-platform approach allows you to reach a wider audience and build a stronger online presence.

By understanding your target audience and actively engaging with them, you can create content that resonates with their needs and preferences. This will not only attract more viewers but also build a loyal and engaged community around your channel. In the next section, we will explore strategies for promoting your channel on social media platforms.

3.2 Promoting Your Channel on Social Media

Social media platforms have become powerful tools for promoting and growing your YouTube channel. With billions of users worldwide, platforms like Facebook, Instagram, Twitter, and TikTok offer immense potential for reaching a wider audience and driving traffic to your videos. In this section, we will explore effective strategies for promoting your channel on social media and maximizing your chances of becoming a YouTube sensation.

3.2.1 Choosing the Right Social Media Platforms

Not all social media platforms are created equal, and it's important to choose the ones that align with your target audience and content niche. Conduct research to identify which platforms your target audience is most active on and focus your efforts there. For example, if your content is primarily visual, platforms like Instagram and Pinterest may be more suitable. If your content is more news or discussion-based, Twitter and Facebook may be better options.

3.2.2 Creating a Consistent Brand Presence

Consistency is key when it comes to promoting your channel on social media. Create a cohesive brand presence across all your social media platforms by using consistent branding elements such as profile pictures, cover photos, and color schemes. This will help your audience recognize and remember your brand, making it easier for them to find and engage with your content.

3.2.3 Sharing Engaging Content

When promoting your channel on social media, it's important to share engaging and valuable content that resonates with your audience. Don't just post links to your videos; instead, create unique and compelling content specifically for each social media platform. This could include behind-the-scenes footage, sneak peeks, teasers, or even short clips from your videos. The goal is to capture your audience's attention and entice them to click through to your YouTube channel.

3.2.4 Utilizing Hashtags and Keywords

Hashtags and keywords play a crucial role in increasing the discoverability of your social media posts. Research popular hashtags and keywords related to your content and incorporate them into your posts. This will help your content appear in relevant search results and reach a wider audience. However, be mindful of using too many hashtags, as it can make your posts appear spammy. Aim for a balance between popular and niche hashtags to maximize your reach.

3.2.5 Engaging with Your Audience

Social media is all about building relationships and engaging with your audience. Take the time to respond to comments, messages, and mentions from your followers. Show genuine interest in their thoughts and opinions, and foster a sense of community around your channel. This will not only help you build a loyal fan base but also encourage your audience to share your content with their own networks, further expanding your reach.

3.2.6 Collaborating with Influencers and Brands

Collaborating with influencers and brands can be a powerful way to promote your channel on social media. Identify influencers or brands within your niche who have a significant following and reach out to them for potential collaborations. This could involve creating joint content, shoutouts, or even sponsored posts. Collaborations can help you tap into new audiences and gain exposure to a wider network of potential subscribers.

3.2.7 Cross-Promoting Your Content

Cross-promotion is another effective strategy for promoting your YouTube channel on social media. Encourage your followers on one platform to follow you on other platforms as well. For example, you can create teaser videos on Instagram or Twitter and direct your audience to watch the full video on YouTube. Additionally, include links to your social media profiles in your YouTube video descriptions and channel banner to make it easy for viewers to connect with you on other platforms.

3.2.8 Utilizing Paid Advertising

While organic promotion is important, utilizing paid advertising on social media can significantly boost your channel's visibility. Platforms like Facebook and Instagram offer targeted advertising options that allow you to reach specific demographics and interests. Consider allocating a portion of your budget to paid advertising campaigns to reach a wider audience and increase your chances of going viral.

3.2.9 Analyzing and Adjusting Your Social Media Strategy

As with any marketing strategy, it's crucial to analyze the performance of your social media efforts and make adjustments accordingly. Utilize the analytics tools provided by each social media platform to track metrics such as engagement, reach, and click-through rates. Identify which types of content perform best and replicate those strategies. Experiment with different posting times, formats, and messaging to optimize your social media promotion strategy.

By effectively promoting your YouTube channel on social media, you can significantly increase your chances of becoming a YouTube sensation. Remember to choose the right platforms, create engaging content, utilize hashtags and keywords, engage with your audience, collaborate with influencers and brands, cross-promote your content, utilize paid advertising, and analyze and adjust your social media strategy. With consistent effort and a well-executed social media promotion plan, you'll be well on your way to achieving YouTube success.

3.3 Collaborating with Other YouTubers

Collaborating with other YouTubers can be a powerful strategy to grow your channel and reach a wider audience. By teaming up with like-minded creators, you can tap into their existing fan base and gain exposure to new viewers who may be interested in your content. In this section, we will explore the benefits of collaborating with other YouTubers and provide you with practical tips on how to find, approach, and build successful collaborative relationships.

3.3.1 The Benefits of Collaboration

Collaborating with other YouTubers offers several advantages that can help accelerate your channel's growth and increase your chances of becoming a YouTube sensation. Here are some key benefits:

1. **Expanded Reach**: When you collaborate with another YouTuber, you have the opportunity to tap into their audience and expose your content to a wider range of viewers. This can lead to an increase in subscribers, views, and engagement on your channel.

2. **Cross-Promotion**: Collaborating allows you to cross-promote each other's channels, giving both parties the chance to gain new subscribers and viewers. By leveraging each other's platforms, you can create a win-win situation where both channels benefit from the collaboration.

3. **Diversification of Content**: Collaborating with other YouTubers can bring fresh perspectives and ideas to your content. It allows you to explore new topics, formats, and styles, which can help keep your channel interesting and engaging for your audience.

4. **Networking Opportunities**: Building relationships with other YouTubers opens doors to networking opportunities within the YouTube community. By connecting with creators in your niche, you can learn from their experiences, share insights, and potentially collaborate on future projects.

3.3.2 Finding and Approaching Potential Collaborators

Finding the right collaborators for your channel is crucial for a successful collaboration. Here are some steps to help you find and approach potential collaborators:

1. **Identify Your Niche**: Start by identifying YouTubers who create content in a similar niche or have an audience that aligns with yours. Look for creators who share similar interests, values, or target demographics.

2. **Research and Evaluate**: Once you have identified potential collaborators, take the time to research their content and audience. Evaluate their channel's engagement, subscriber count, and overall reputation to ensure they align with your goals and values.

3. **Reach Out**: Once you have identified potential collaborators, reach out to them with a personalized message expressing your interest in collaborating. Be genuine, concise, and highlight how a collaboration could benefit both parties. It's important to show that you have done your research and understand their content.

4. **Provide Value**: When approaching potential collaborators, make sure to emphasize how you can provide value to their channel and audience. Highlight your unique skills, expertise, or ideas that can contribute to a successful collaboration.

5. **Be Professional and Respectful**: When reaching out to potential collaborators, maintain a professional and respectful tone. Remember that they may receive numerous collaboration requests, so it's important to stand out by being polite, concise, and professional in your communication.

3.3.3 Planning and Executing Collaborative Projects

Once you have found a collaborator and they have expressed interest in working with you, it's time to plan and execute the collaborative project. Here are some steps to help you navigate the process:

1. **Define the Objective**: Clearly define the objective of the collaboration. Determine what you want to achieve, whether it's creating a joint video, hosting a live stream, or collaborating on a series of videos. Establishing a clear objective will help guide the planning and execution process.

2. **Brainstorm Ideas**: Collaborate with your partner to brainstorm ideas for the collaborative project. Consider the interests and preferences of both audiences and aim to create content that will resonate with both sets of viewers. Be open to compromise and find a balance that showcases both creators' strengths.

3. **Establish Roles and Responsibilities**: Clearly define the roles and responsibilities of each collaborator. Determine who will be responsible for scripting, filming, editing, and promoting the collaborative content. Establishing clear roles will help ensure a smooth workflow and avoid any confusion or misunderstandings.

4. **Set Deadlines**: Establish a timeline for the collaborative project and set deadlines for each stage of the process. This will help keep both parties accountable and ensure that the project stays on track. Effective communication and regular check-ins are essential to meet the established deadlines.

5. **Collaborate on Content Creation**: Work closely with your collaborator throughout the content creation process. Share ideas, provide feedback, and collaborate on scripting, storyboarding, and editing. Aim to create content that showcases the strengths of both creators and provides value to both audiences.

3.3.4 Cross-Promoting Each Other's Channels

Cross-promotion is a key aspect of collaborating with other YouTubers. Here are some strategies to effectively cross-promote each other's channels:

1. **Feature Each Other in Videos**: Create videos where you feature each other's channels and content. This can be done through shout-outs, collaborations, or guest appearances. By introducing your audience to your collaborator, you can encourage them to check out their channel and subscribe.
2. **Create Playlists**: Collaborate on creating playlists that feature each other's videos. This allows viewers to easily navigate between your channels and discover more of your content. Make sure to promote these playlists on your channel and encourage your viewers to explore them.
3. **Promote on Social Media**: Utilize your social media platforms to promote your collaborative content. Share teasers, behind-the-scenes footage, or snippets of the collaboration to generate excitement and drive traffic to both channels.
4. **Engage with Each Other's Audience**: Take the time to engage with your collaborator's audience by responding to comments, answering questions, and showing genuine interest in their viewers. This will help foster a sense of community and encourage viewers to explore both channels.

3.3.5 Building Long-Term Collaborative Relationships

Building long-term collaborative relationships can be beneficial for both parties involved. Here are some tips to foster successful long-term collaborations:

1. **Maintain Communication**: Regularly communicate with your collaborator to discuss future projects, ideas, and opportunities. Effective communication is key to building a strong collaborative relationship.
2. **Evaluate and Learn**: After each collaboration, take the time to evaluate the success of the project and learn from the experience. Identify what worked well and areas for improvement. Use this feedback to refine your future collaborations and make them even more successful.
3. **Support Each Other**: Show support for your collaborator's individual projects by promoting their content, engaging with their audience, and providing feedback. Building a supportive relationship will strengthen your collaboration and create a positive environment for future projects.
4. **Explore New Opportunities**: Be open to exploring new opportunities and formats for collaboration. Consider branching out into different types of content, such as podcasts, live streams, or joint merchandise. Continuously innovating and experimenting will keep your collaborations fresh and exciting.

Collaborating with other YouTubers can be a game-changer for your channel's growth and success. By leveraging the power of collaboration, you can tap into new audiences, diversify your content, and build valuable relationships within the YouTube community. Remember to approach collaborations with professionalism, provide value to your collaborators, and focus on creating content that resonates with both sets of viewers. With the right approach and mindset, collaborating with other YouTubers can help you become a YouTube sensation in no time.

3.4 Engaging with Your Viewers

Engaging with your viewers is a crucial aspect of building a successful YouTube channel. When you actively interact with your audience, it not only strengthens the connection between you and your viewers but also helps in building a loyal community. Engaging with your viewers can lead to increased watch time, higher engagement rates, and ultimately, more subscribers. In this section, we will explore some effective strategies to engage with your viewers and create a thriving community around your channel.

3.4.1 Responding to Comments

One of the simplest yet most effective ways to engage with your viewers is by responding to their comments. When viewers take the time to leave a comment on your video, it shows that they are actively interested in your content. By responding to their comments, you acknowledge their presence and make them feel valued.

Make it a habit to regularly check the comments section of your videos and respond to as many comments as possible. You can start by replying to comments that ask questions or provide feedback. Engage in meaningful conversations with your viewers and show genuine interest in their thoughts and opinions. This not only encourages more comments but also creates a sense of community on your channel.

3.4.2 Hosting Live Q&A Sessions

Hosting live Q&A sessions is an excellent way to directly engage with your viewers in real-time. These sessions allow your audience to ask you questions and receive immediate responses. Live Q&A sessions can be conducted through YouTube's live streaming feature or other platforms like Instagram or Facebook Live.

Promote your live Q&A session in advance to generate interest and ensure a good turnout. Encourage your viewers to submit their questions beforehand or during the live session. During the session, make sure to address each question and provide detailed answers. Engaging in live conversations with your viewers not only strengthens your relationship with them but also helps in creating a sense of community among your audience.

3.4.3 Creating Polls and Surveys

Another effective way to engage with your viewers is by creating polls and surveys. These interactive tools allow you to gather feedback, opinions, and preferences from your audience. Polls and surveys can be created using YouTube's Community tab, social media platforms, or external survey tools.

Use polls to ask your viewers about their favorite topics, video ideas, or any other relevant questions. Surveys can be used to gather more detailed feedback on your content, channel branding, or any other aspect you want to improve. Analyze the results of your polls and surveys and consider implementing changes based on the feedback received. By involving your viewers in decision-making processes, you make them feel valued and increase their sense of ownership in your channel.

3.4.4 Featuring Viewer Content

Featuring viewer content is an excellent way to showcase the talent and creativity of your audience. Encourage your viewers to submit their own videos, artwork, or any other content related to your channel's niche. Select the best submissions and feature them in your videos or dedicate separate videos to showcase viewer content.

By featuring viewer content, you not only engage with your audience but also provide them with a platform to gain exposure and recognition. This creates a sense of community and encourages other viewers to participate and contribute their own content. Make sure to give proper credit to the creators and provide links to their channels or social media profiles.

3.4.5 Hosting Giveaways and Contests

Hosting giveaways and contests is a fun and engaging way to reward your viewers and encourage their participation. You can organize giveaways where viewers have a chance to win merchandise, exclusive content, or any other relevant prizes. Contests can involve challenges or creative tasks related to your channel's niche.

Promote your giveaways and contests through your videos, social media platforms, and other channels. Set clear rules and guidelines for participation and announce the winners publicly. Giveaways and contests not only create excitement among your viewers but also attract new subscribers and increase engagement on your channel.

3.4.6 Engaging on Social Media

In addition to engaging with your viewers on YouTube, it is essential to extend your presence to other social media platforms. Create accounts on platforms like Instagram, Twitter, Facebook, or TikTok, depending on your target audience. Use these platforms to share behind-the-scenes content, updates, and interact with your viewers.

Respond to comments, direct messages, and mentions on social media platforms. Engage in conversations, ask questions, and encourage your followers to share their thoughts and opinions. By actively participating in social media discussions, you not only strengthen your relationship with your existing viewers but also attract new ones.

3.4.7 Hosting Meetups and Fan Events

As your channel grows, consider hosting meetups or fan events to connect with your viewers in person. These events provide a unique opportunity to meet your audience, take photos, sign autographs, and have meaningful conversations. Meetups and fan events can be organized in collaboration with other YouTubers or as standalone events.

Promote your meetups and fan events well in advance through your videos, social media platforms, and website. Ensure that the event details are clear and easily accessible. Meeting your viewers face-to-face not only strengthens your bond with them but also creates a memorable experience that they will cherish.

Engaging with your viewers is an ongoing process that requires consistent effort and dedication. By responding to comments, hosting live sessions, creating polls, featuring viewer content, hosting giveaways, engaging on social media, and hosting meetups, you can build a strong and loyal community around your YouTube channel. Remember, the more you engage with your viewers, the more they will feel connected to your content and the more likely they are to become loyal subscribers.

3.5 Utilizing SEO for Discoverability

In the vast sea of YouTube videos, it's crucial to optimize your content for search engines to increase its discoverability. Search Engine Optimization (SEO) plays a significant role in helping your videos rank higher in search results and attract more viewers. By implementing effective SEO strategies, you can improve your chances of becoming a YouTube sensation. In this section, we will explore various techniques to utilize SEO for discoverability and maximize your video's reach.

3.5.1 Keyword Research

Keyword research is the foundation of SEO. It involves identifying the words and phrases that people commonly use when searching for content related to your niche. By incorporating these keywords into your video titles, descriptions, and tags, you can increase the likelihood of your videos appearing in relevant search results.

To conduct keyword research, start by brainstorming a list of potential keywords that are relevant to your video content. You can use tools like Google Keyword Planner, SEMrush, or TubeBuddy to find popular keywords and analyze their search volume and competition. Look for keywords that have a high search volume but relatively low competition to optimize your chances of ranking well.

Once you have a list of keywords, strategically incorporate them into your video titles, descriptions, and tags. However, avoid keyword stuffing, as it can negatively impact your video's visibility. Instead, aim for a natural and balanced use of keywords that accurately represent your video's content.

3.5.2 Optimizing Video Titles, Descriptions, and Tags

When it comes to optimizing your videos for search engines, the title, description, and tags are crucial elements to focus on. These components provide valuable information to both viewers and search engines, helping them understand the content of your video.

Video Titles

Crafting compelling and keyword-rich video titles is essential for attracting viewers and improving search rankings. Your title should accurately reflect the content of your video while also being attention-grabbing. Consider using numbers, intriguing adjectives, or posing questions to make your titles more enticing.

Include your primary keyword or key phrase in the title, preferably towards the beginning. This helps search engines understand the relevance of your video to specific search queries. However, ensure that your title remains concise and easy to understand.

Video Descriptions

Video descriptions provide an opportunity to provide more context and information about your video. Aim to write detailed and engaging descriptions that not only include your primary keyword but also provide additional relevant keywords and phrases.

Incorporate a brief summary of your video's content, along with any relevant links, social media handles, or timestamps for specific sections within the video. This information helps viewers understand what to expect from your video and encourages them to watch it.

Video Tags

Tags are another crucial element for optimizing your videos' discoverability. They help YouTube's algorithm understand the content of your video and categorize it appropriately. Include a mix of broad and specific tags that accurately represent the topics covered in your video.

Consider using variations of your primary keyword, related keywords, and phrases as tags. Additionally, analyze the tags used by popular videos in your niche to gain insights and inspiration for your own tags. However, avoid using irrelevant or misleading tags, as it can harm your video's visibility and credibility.

3.5.3 Closed Captions and Transcriptions

Closed captions and transcriptions not only make your videos more accessible to viewers with hearing impairments but also contribute to SEO. YouTube's algorithm can crawl through the text in closed captions and transcriptions, providing additional context and keywords for search rankings.

Ensure that your videos have accurate and well-timed closed captions. You can either manually create them or use YouTube's automatic captioning feature, which you can then edit for accuracy. Additionally, consider providing a full transcription of your video in the description or as a separate document. This allows search engines to index the text and improve your video's discoverability.

3.5.4 Engaging Thumbnails

Thumbnails are the first visual impression viewers have of your video, and they play a significant role in attracting clicks and improving search rankings. Create visually appealing and engaging thumbnails that accurately represent the content of your video.

Include relevant text, images, or graphics in your thumbnails to make them stand out. Use contrasting colors and bold fonts to make the text easily readable. Additionally, consider adding an element of curiosity or intrigue to entice viewers to click on your video.

3.5.5 Cross-Promotion and Backlinking

Cross-promotion and backlinking are effective strategies to improve your video's discoverability and SEO. Collaborate with other YouTubers or influencers in your niche to create videos together or feature each other's content. This not only exposes your channel to a wider audience but also generates backlinks to your videos, which can positively impact search rankings.

Additionally, promote your videos on your website, blog, or other social media platforms. Embed your videos in relevant blog posts or articles and share them across your social media channels. This increases the visibility of your videos and encourages viewers to engage with your content.

3.5.6 Monitoring and Analytics

Regularly monitor your video's performance and analyze the data provided by YouTube's analytics. Pay attention to metrics such as watch time, audience retention, click-through rate, and engagement. This data can help you understand how viewers are discovering and interacting with your videos.

Identify trends and patterns in your analytics to refine your SEO strategies. Determine which keywords, titles, or descriptions are performing well and replicate their success in future videos. Additionally, use the analytics data to identify areas for improvement and make data-driven decisions to optimize your content for better discoverability.

By implementing these SEO strategies, you can significantly improve the discoverability of your YouTube videos. Remember to conduct thorough keyword research, optimize your video titles, descriptions, and tags, utilize closed captions and transcriptions, create engaging thumbnails, cross-promote and backlink, and monitor your video's performance through analytics. With consistent effort and optimization, you can increase your chances of becoming a YouTube sensation in no time.

3.6 Analyzing and Utilizing YouTube Analytics

Once you have started creating and uploading videos on your YouTube channel, it is crucial to analyze and utilize YouTube Analytics to understand your audience, track your channel's performance, and make data-driven decisions to optimize your content strategy. YouTube Analytics provides valuable insights into your viewers' behavior, demographics, and engagement metrics, allowing you to tailor your content to meet their preferences and interests. In this section, we will explore how to effectively analyze and utilize YouTube Analytics to grow your channel and become a YouTube sensation.

3.6.1 Understanding YouTube Analytics

YouTube Analytics is a powerful tool that provides comprehensive data about your channel's performance. To access YouTube Analytics, go to your YouTube Studio dashboard and click on the "Analytics" tab. Here, you will find a wealth of information about your channel, including:

3.6.1.1 Overview

The Overview section gives you a snapshot of your channel's performance over a selected time period. It provides key metrics such as views, watch time, subscribers gained or lost, and estimated revenue. This section also includes a graph that visualizes your channel's performance trends.

3.6.1.2 Reach

The Reach section provides insights into how your videos are discovered and viewed. It includes metrics such as impressions, click-through rate (CTR), and average view duration. Understanding these metrics can help you optimize your video titles, thumbnails, and descriptions to attract more viewers.

3.6.1.3 Engagement

The Engagement section focuses on how viewers interact with your content. It includes metrics such as likes, dislikes, comments, and shares. By analyzing these metrics, you can identify which videos resonate the most with your audience and create more engaging content in the future.

3.6.1.4 Audience

The Audience section provides demographic information about your viewers, including their age, gender, and geographic location. This data can help you understand your target audience better and tailor your content to their preferences.

3.6.1.5 Revenue

The Revenue section displays your estimated earnings from ads on your videos. It also provides insights into the monetization status of your channel and the performance of different ad formats.

3.6.2 Analyzing YouTube Analytics

Now that you understand the different sections of YouTube Analytics, let's dive into how to effectively analyze the data to gain valuable insights.

3.6.2.1 Identify Top-Performing Videos

Start by identifying your top-performing videos based on metrics such as views, watch time, and engagement. Look for patterns and commonalities among these videos. What topics, formats, or styles resonate the most with your audience? Use this information to guide your content creation strategy and focus on producing more of what works.

3.6.2.2 Understand Audience Behavior

Analyze the audience retention graph in the Reach section to understand how viewers engage with your videos. Are there specific points in your videos where viewers drop off? This can indicate areas where you need to improve your content or make it more engaging. Additionally, pay attention to the average view duration metric to gauge how long viewers are watching your videos. If you notice a significant drop-off in view duration, consider making your videos more concise and engaging.

3.6.2.3 Explore Audience Demographics

The Audience section provides valuable demographic information about your viewers. Use this data to understand who your target audience is and tailor your content to their preferences. For example, if you discover that a significant portion of your audience is in a specific age group, create content that appeals to that demographic.

3.6.2.4 Track Channel Growth

Monitor the growth of your channel by tracking metrics such as subscribers gained or lost, views, and watch time. Set realistic milestones and targets for your channel's growth and evaluate your progress regularly. If you notice a decline in any of these metrics, analyze the factors that may have contributed to it and make adjustments to your content strategy accordingly.

3.6.3 Utilizing YouTube Analytics

Analyzing YouTube Analytics is only valuable if you use the insights to optimize your content strategy and improve your channel's performance. Here are some ways to utilize YouTube Analytics effectively:

3.6.3.1 Content Optimization

Use the data from YouTube Analytics to optimize your content. Identify the topics, formats, and styles that resonate the most with your audience and create more of that content. Pay attention to the audience retention graph and average view duration to make your videos more engaging and retain viewers for longer.

3.6.3.2 Audience Targeting

Leverage the demographic information in the Audience section to target your content to specific audience segments. Create videos that cater to the preferences and interests of your target audience, increasing the likelihood of engagement and sharing.

3.6.3.3 Collaboration Opportunities

Identify potential collaboration opportunities by analyzing the audience demographics of other successful YouTubers in your niche. Look for creators whose audience aligns with yours and reach out to them for collaboration. Collaborating with other YouTubers can help you tap into their audience and expand your reach.

3.6.3.4 Experimentation and Iteration

YouTube Analytics provides valuable feedback on your content's performance. Use this feedback to experiment with different video formats, topics, and styles. Continuously iterate and improve your content based on the insights gained from YouTube Analytics.

By regularly analyzing and utilizing YouTube Analytics, you can gain a deep understanding of your audience, optimize your content strategy, and make data-driven decisions to grow your channel. Remember, consistency and adaptability are key to becoming a YouTube sensation.

4 Optimizing Your Channel

4.1 Creating an Eye-Catching Channel Banner

Your channel banner is one of the first things viewers see when they visit your YouTube channel. It serves as a visual representation of your brand and can greatly impact a viewer's first impression. Creating an eye-catching channel banner is essential to attracting and retaining viewers. In this section, we will discuss the key elements of a compelling channel banner and provide step-by-step instructions on how to create one.

4.1.1 Understanding the Importance of a Channel Banner

Before diving into the process of creating a channel banner, it's important to understand why it is crucial for your YouTube success. Your channel banner is like the cover of a book - it needs to grab attention and entice viewers to explore your content further. A well-designed banner can help you establish your brand identity, convey your channel's theme, and make a lasting impression on your audience.

4.1.2 Defining Your Channel's Branding

Before you start designing your channel banner, it's essential to have a clear understanding of your channel's branding. Your branding should reflect your channel's niche, target audience, and overall message. Take some time to define your channel's unique selling points and core values. This will help you create a channel banner that aligns with your brand identity.

4.1.3 Choosing the Right Dimensions

YouTube recommends using a channel banner with dimensions of 2560 x 1440 pixels. However, keep in mind that the banner will be displayed differently on various devices. To ensure your banner looks great across all platforms, it's important to consider the safe area, which is the visible portion of the banner on different devices. The safe area is approximately 1546 x 423 pixels, with the center 1546 x 423 pixels being the most important.

4.1.4 Designing Your Channel Banner

Now that you have a clear understanding of your channel's branding and the dimensions for your banner, it's time to start designing. Here are some steps to help you create an eye-catching channel banner:

1. Choose a visually appealing background: Select a background that complements your channel's theme and captures the attention of viewers. You can use high-quality images, patterns, or solid colors as your background.
2. Incorporate your channel's name and logo: Include your channel's name and logo in a prominent position on the banner. This helps viewers easily identify your channel and reinforces your brand.
3. Use captivating visuals: Add visually appealing elements such as images, illustrations, or icons that represent your channel's content. These visuals should be relevant to your niche and help convey your channel's message.
4. Include a tagline or slogan: Consider adding a tagline or slogan that summarizes your channel's value proposition. This can help viewers understand what your channel is about and why they should subscribe.
5. Use fonts that are easy to read: Choose fonts that are legible and align with your channel's branding. Avoid using overly decorative or hard-to-read fonts, as they can make your banner appear cluttered and unprofessional.
6. Maintain consistency with your brand colors: Use colors that are consistent with your channel's branding. This helps create a cohesive and visually appealing banner that aligns with your overall brand identity.
7. Optimize for mobile devices: Keep in mind that a significant portion of YouTube viewers access the platform through mobile devices.

Ensure that your banner looks great on smaller screens by avoiding text or important elements near the edges.

4.1.5 Testing and Optimizing Your Channel Banner

Once you have designed your channel banner, it's important to test it across different devices and screen sizes to ensure it looks great everywhere. Ask friends or fellow YouTubers to provide feedback on your banner and make any necessary adjustments.

Additionally, consider periodically updating your channel banner to keep it fresh and engaging. This can help maintain viewer interest and attract new viewers to your channel.

4.1.6 Uploading Your Channel Banner

To upload your channel banner, follow these steps:

1. Sign in to your YouTube account and go to your channel page.
2. Click on the "Customize Channel" button.
3. Hover over the area where your channel banner will appear and click on the pencil icon that appears.
4. Select "Edit channel art" from the dropdown menu.
5. Choose the image file of your channel banner from your computer and click "Open."
6. Adjust the positioning of your banner if necessary.
7. Click "Select" to save your changes.

Congratulations! You have successfully created and uploaded an eye-catching channel banner for your YouTube channel. Remember to regularly review and update your banner to reflect any changes in your branding or channel focus. A visually appealing and well-designed channel banner can help attract viewers and make a positive first impression, setting the stage for your YouTube success.

4.2 Writing Effective Channel Descriptions

Your channel description is one of the first things viewers see when they visit your YouTube channel. It serves as a brief introduction to your content and can play a crucial role in attracting and retaining subscribers. Writing an effective channel description is essential for creating a strong brand identity and enticing viewers to explore your videos further. In this section, we will discuss the key elements of a compelling channel description and provide step-by-step guidance on how to write one that captures the attention of your target audience.

4.2.1 Understanding the Purpose of a Channel Description

Before diving into the process of writing an effective channel description, it's important to understand its purpose. A channel description serves as a snapshot of your content and provides viewers with an overview of what they can expect from your channel. It should be concise, engaging, and informative, giving viewers a reason to subscribe and explore your videos further.

4.2.2 Identifying Your Unique Selling Proposition

To write an effective channel description, you need to identify your unique selling proposition (USP). Your USP is what sets you apart from other creators in your niche and gives viewers a reason to choose your channel over others. Consider what makes your content unique, whether it's your expertise, personality, or the specific niche you cater to. Understanding your USP will help you craft a channel description that highlights your strengths and appeals to your target audience.

4.2.3 Crafting a Compelling Introduction

The first few sentences of your channel description are crucial in capturing the attention of viewers. Craft a compelling introduction that immediately grabs their interest and entices them to continue reading. Start by introducing yourself or your brand and briefly explain what your channel is all about. Use concise and engaging language to create a strong first impression.

4.2.4 Highlighting Your Content and Value Proposition

After the introduction, it's time to highlight the content you offer and the value it provides to viewers. Clearly communicate the type of videos you create, the topics you cover, and the benefits viewers can expect from watching your content. Focus on the value you provide, whether it's entertainment, education, inspiration, or a combination of these. Use persuasive language to convince viewers that your channel is worth their time and subscription.

4.2.5 Showcasing Your Expertise and Credibility

Establishing your expertise and credibility is essential in gaining the trust of your audience. If you have relevant qualifications, certifications, or experience in your niche, mention them in your channel description. This will help viewers understand why they should trust your content and consider you an authority in your field. Additionally, if you have been featured in media outlets or have received any notable recognition, include that information as well.

4.2.6 Incorporating Keywords for Discoverability

To improve the discoverability of your channel, it's important to incorporate relevant keywords in your channel description. Conduct keyword research to identify the terms and phrases that your target audience is likely to search for.

Include these keywords naturally throughout your description, but avoid keyword stuffing, as it can make your description sound unnatural and spammy. By optimizing your channel description with keywords, you increase the chances of your channel appearing in search results.

4.2.7 Formatting and Organization

A well-formatted and organized channel description is easier to read and navigate. Use paragraphs and bullet points to break up the text and make it more visually appealing. Consider using subheadings to categorize different sections of your description, such as "About Me," "Content Categories," or "Upcoming Projects." This helps viewers quickly find the information they are looking for and makes your channel description more user-friendly.

4.2.8 Call-to-Action and Contact Information

Don't forget to include a call-to-action (CTA) in your channel description. Encourage viewers to subscribe to your channel, like your videos, and engage with your content. You can also direct them to other platforms where they can connect with you, such as your website, social media accounts, or email newsletter. Including your contact information, such as an email address or business inquiries, allows potential collaborators or sponsors to reach out to you easily.

4.2.9 Regularly Updating Your Channel Description

As your channel grows and evolves, it's important to regularly update your channel description to reflect any changes. This could include new content categories, collaborations, or milestones you have achieved. By keeping your channel description up to date, you show viewers that your channel is active and continuously improving.

4.2.10 Reviewing and Refining Your Channel Description

After writing your channel description, take the time to review and refine it. Read it aloud to ensure it flows smoothly and sounds engaging. Check for any grammatical or spelling errors and make sure the tone and language align with your brand identity. Consider seeking feedback from others, such as friends, family, or fellow creators, to get different perspectives and suggestions for improvement.

Writing an effective channel description is a crucial step in attracting and retaining subscribers on YouTube. By understanding the purpose of a channel description, identifying your unique selling proposition, and crafting a compelling introduction, you can create a description that captures the attention of your target audience. Remember to highlight your content and value proposition, showcase your expertise and credibility, and incorporate keywords for discoverability. Format and organize your description for readability, include a call-to-action and contact information, and regularly update and refine it as your channel grows. With a well-written channel description, you can make a strong impression on viewers and increase the chances of turning them into loyal subscribers.

4.3 Organizing Your Video Playlists

Once you have started creating and uploading videos to your YouTube channel, it's important to organize them in a way that makes it easy for your viewers to find and navigate through your content. This is where video playlists come in. Playlists allow you to group related videos together, creating a seamless viewing experience for your audience. In this section, we will explore the importance of organizing your video playlists and provide you with step-by-step instructions on how to create and optimize them for maximum impact.

4.3.1 Why Organize Your Video Playlists?

Organizing your video playlists is crucial for several reasons. Firstly, it helps your viewers discover more of your content. When a viewer finishes watching one of your videos, they are more likely to continue watching if they see a playlist of related videos that pique their interest. By grouping similar videos together, you increase the chances of viewers staying on your channel and consuming more of your content.

Secondly, playlists improve the overall user experience on your channel. Instead of having viewers search through your entire video library to find specific topics or series, playlists provide a curated selection of videos that are relevant to their interests. This saves them time and effort, making them more likely to engage with your content and subscribe to your channel.

Lastly, organizing your video playlists can have a positive impact on your channel's search engine optimization (SEO). YouTube's algorithm takes into account the engagement and watch time of your videos when determining their ranking in search results. By keeping viewers engaged with your content through playlists, you increase the likelihood of higher watch times and improved search rankings.

4.3.2 Creating and Optimizing Your Video Playlists

Now that you understand the importance of organizing your video playlists, let's dive into the step-by-step process of creating and optimizing them for maximum impact.

Step 1: Identify Themes or Categories

Before creating your playlists, it's important to identify the themes or categories that your videos fall into. This will help you group your videos in a logical and organized manner. For example, if you have a beauty channel, you might have playlists for makeup tutorials, skincare routines, and product reviews.

Step 2: Create New Playlists

To create a new playlist, log in to your YouTube account and navigate to your channel's homepage. Click on the "Playlists" tab and then click on the "New Playlist" button. Give your playlist a descriptive and engaging title that accurately represents the content it contains.

Step 3: Add Videos to Your Playlists

Once you have created a playlist, it's time to add videos to it. To do this, go to the video you want to add and click on the "Add to" button below the video player. Select the playlist you want to add the video to from the drop-down menu. You can add multiple videos to a playlist at once by selecting the checkbox next to each video and clicking on the "Add to" button.

Step 4: Optimize Your Playlist Settings

After adding videos to your playlist, it's important to optimize its settings to enhance the viewing experience for your audience. Click on the three dots next to the playlist title and select "Playlist settings." Here, you can customize the playlist's title, description, and thumbnail. Make sure to write a compelling and keyword-rich description that accurately describes the content of the playlist.

Step 5: Arrange Videos in a Logical Order

To ensure a seamless viewing experience, arrange the videos in your playlist in a logical order. You can do this by clicking and dragging the videos into the desired position within the playlist. Consider the flow of the content and arrange the videos in a way that makes sense to your viewers.

Step 6: Promote Your Playlists

Once you have created and optimized your playlists, it's time to promote them to your audience. Include links to your playlists in your video descriptions, end screens, and cards. Additionally, consider featuring your playlists on your channel's homepage to make them easily accessible to new viewers.

4.3.3 Best Practices for Video Playlists

To make the most out of your video playlists, here are some best practices to keep in mind:

- Regularly update and add new videos to your playlists to keep them fresh and engaging.
- Use eye-catching thumbnails for your playlists to attract viewers' attention.
- Include relevant keywords in your playlist titles and descriptions to improve search visibility.
- Consider creating a series playlist for recurring content to make it easy for viewers to binge-watch.
- Collaborate with other YouTubers by featuring their videos in your playlists and vice versa.
- Monitor the performance of your playlists using YouTube Analytics to identify which ones are resonating with your audience and make adjustments accordingly.

By organizing your video playlists effectively, you can enhance the viewing experience for your audience, increase engagement, and improve your channel's overall performance. Take the time to create and optimize your playlists, and you'll be on your way to becoming a YouTube sensation in no time.

Remember, consistency and quality content are key to building a loyal and engaged audience. So keep creating, optimizing, and organizing your videos, and watch your channel grow!

4.4 Customizing Your Channel Layout

Once you have created a compelling channel brand and organized your video playlists, it's time to customize your channel layout. Customizing your channel layout not only enhances the visual appeal of your channel but also helps you showcase your content in a way that is engaging and user-friendly for your viewers. In this section, we will explore various ways to customize your channel layout to make it stand out and attract more viewers.

4.4.1 Channel Art and Logo

The first step in customizing your channel layout is to create eye-catching channel art and a logo. Channel art is the large banner that appears at the top of your channel page, while the logo is a smaller image that represents your channel across YouTube. These visual elements are crucial for branding and creating a memorable identity for your channel.

When designing your channel art, consider using high-quality images that reflect the theme or niche of your channel. You can include your channel name, tagline, or any other relevant information to make it more informative. Ensure that the text is legible and the overall design is visually appealing.

Your channel logo should be simple, recognizable, and easily identifiable even at smaller sizes. It should be consistent with your channel's branding and reflect the essence of your content. You can use graphic design tools or hire a professional designer to create a logo that aligns with your channel's identity.

4.4.2 Featured Video and Channel Trailer

Another way to customize your channel layout is by featuring a video or a channel trailer. A featured video is a video that automatically plays when someone visits your channel, while a channel trailer is a short video that introduces new viewers to your channel and encourages them to subscribe.

Choose a video that represents your channel's best content or showcases what your channel is all about. It should be engaging, informative, and leave a lasting impression on your viewers. If you decide to create a channel trailer, keep it concise and captivating, highlighting the unique aspects of your channel and why viewers should subscribe.

To set a featured video or channel trailer, go to your YouTube Studio dashboard, click on the "Customization" tab, and select "Featured content." From there, you can choose the video you want to feature or upload a new one.

4.4.3 Sections and Playlists

Organizing your channel's content into sections and playlists is an effective way to customize your channel layout and make it easier for viewers to navigate through your videos. Sections allow you to group similar videos together, while playlists enable you to curate a collection of videos based on a specific theme or topic.

To create sections, go to your YouTube Studio dashboard, click on the "Customization" tab, and select "Sections." You can choose from various section types such as "Popular uploads," "Recent uploads," or create custom sections based on your preferences. Rearrange the sections to prioritize the content you want to highlight.

Creating playlists is equally important as it helps viewers discover more of your content and encourages them to stay on your channel for longer. Group related videos into playlists and give them descriptive titles that accurately represent the content within. You can also add custom thumbnails to make your playlists visually appealing.

4.4.4 Channel Navigation and About Section

Customizing your channel's navigation and about section is essential for providing important information to your viewers and making it easy for them to explore your content. The navigation menu appears below your channel art and allows viewers to access different sections of your channel, such as videos, playlists, and community.

To customize your channel's navigation, go to your YouTube Studio dashboard, click on the "Customization" tab, and select "Layout." From there, you can choose which sections to display in your navigation menu and rearrange them according to your preference.

The about section is where you can provide a brief description of your channel, including what your content is about, your upload schedule, and any other relevant information. It's also a great place to include links to your social media profiles or website. To edit your channel's about section, go to your YouTube Studio dashboard, click on the "Customization" tab, and select "Basic info."

4.4.5 Channel Trailer Autoplay and Featured Channels

In addition to customizing your channel layout, you can also enable channel trailer autoplay and feature other channels on your page. Enabling channel trailer autoplay ensures that new viewers are immediately introduced to your channel's content when they visit your page. This can significantly increase the chances of them subscribing to your channel.

To enable channel trailer autoplay, go to your YouTube Studio dashboard, click on the "Customization" tab, and select "Channel trailer." From there, you can toggle the autoplay feature on or off.

Featuring other channels on your page is a great way to collaborate with fellow YouTubers and cross-promote each other's content. You can choose channels that align with your niche or have a similar target audience. To feature other channels, go to your YouTube Studio dashboard, click on the "Customization" tab, and select "Featured channels."

By customizing your channel layout, you can create a visually appealing and user-friendly experience for your viewers. Remember to regularly update your channel art, featured video, and playlists to keep your channel fresh and engaging. A well-customized channel layout not only attracts more viewers but also helps in building a strong brand presence on YouTube.

5 Monetizing Your Channel

5.1 Understanding YouTube's Partner Program

In order to monetize your YouTube channel and start earning money from your videos, it is important to understand YouTube's Partner Program. This program allows creators to earn revenue through advertisements that are displayed on their videos. In this section, we will explore the requirements, benefits, and strategies for maximizing your earnings through the YouTube Partner Program.

5.1.1 Requirements for Joining the Partner Program

Before you can start monetizing your videos, you need to meet certain requirements set by YouTube. These requirements include:

1. **Eligibility**: To be eligible for the YouTube Partner Program, you need to have at least 1,000 subscribers on your channel and have accumulated 4,000 watch hours in the past 12 months.
2. **Adherence to YouTube's Policies**: Your channel must comply with YouTube's Community Guidelines and Terms of Service. It is important to create original content and avoid any copyright infringements or violations.
3. **AdSense Account**: You need to have an AdSense account linked to your YouTube channel. AdSense is Google's advertising platform that allows you to earn money from ads displayed on your videos.

Once you meet these requirements, you can apply to join the YouTube Partner Program through your YouTube Studio account. It is important to note that meeting the requirements does not guarantee acceptance into the program. YouTube reviews each application to ensure that the channel meets their guidelines and policies.

5.1.2 Benefits of the Partner Program

Joining the YouTube Partner Program offers several benefits to creators. These benefits include:

1. **Monetization**: The primary benefit of the Partner Program is the ability to monetize your videos. By enabling ads on your videos, you can earn money based on the number of views and ad interactions.
2. **Access to Premium Features**: Being a YouTube Partner gives you access to additional features such as custom thumbnails, external annotations, and the ability to link to external websites through end screens.
3. **YouTube Premium Revenue**: As a Partner, you also have the opportunity to earn a share of the revenue generated from YouTube Premium subscribers who watch your content.
4. **Creator Support**: YouTube provides support to its Partners through resources, workshops, and access to the Creator Academy. This support can help you improve your content, grow your audience, and increase your earnings.

5.1.3 Maximizing Earnings through the Partner Program

While joining the YouTube Partner Program is a significant milestone, it is important to implement strategies to maximize your earnings. Here are some tips to help you make the most out of the Partner Program:

1. **Optimize Ad Placement**: Experiment with different ad placements to find the most effective positions for ads on your videos. Strategic ad placement can increase viewer engagement and maximize your ad revenue.
2. **Focus on Watch Time**: YouTube prioritizes watch time when determining the success of a video. Create longer videos that keep viewers engaged and encourage them to watch until the end. This will increase your watch time and potentially lead to higher ad revenue.

3. **Diversify Revenue Streams**: While ads are the primary source of revenue through the Partner Program, consider exploring alternative revenue streams such as merchandise sales, sponsored content, or crowdfunding. Diversifying your income can help you generate more revenue and reduce reliance on ad revenue alone.
4. **Engage with Your Audience**: Building a loyal and engaged audience is crucial for long-term success on YouTube. Respond to comments, ask for feedback, and create content that resonates with your viewers. Engaged viewers are more likely to watch your videos in full and interact with the ads displayed.
5. **Stay Updated with YouTube Policies**: YouTube's policies and guidelines are subject to change. Stay informed about any updates or changes to ensure that your channel remains compliant. Violations of YouTube's policies can result in demonetization or even the termination of your channel.

By understanding the requirements, benefits, and strategies for maximizing your earnings through the YouTube Partner Program, you can take the necessary steps to monetize your channel and start earning money from your videos. Remember, building a successful YouTube channel takes time, dedication, and consistent effort.

5.2 Enabling and Optimizing Ads on Your Videos

Once you have started creating engaging content and building an audience on YouTube, it's time to explore the various ways to monetize your channel. One of the most common and effective methods is through enabling and optimizing ads on your videos. In this section, we will guide you through the process of setting up ads on your channel and maximizing your revenue potential.

5.2.1 Understanding YouTube's Ad Formats

Before diving into the process of enabling ads on your videos, it's important to understand the different ad formats available on YouTube. This knowledge will help you make informed decisions about which ad formats to enable and how they can impact your viewers' experience.

1. **Skippable Video Ads**: These ads allow viewers to skip the ad after 5 seconds. As a creator, you earn revenue when viewers watch the entire ad or at least 30 seconds of it, whichever is shorter.
2. **Non-Skippable Video Ads**: These ads cannot be skipped by viewers and typically appear before, during, or after your video. You earn revenue when viewers watch the entire ad.
3. **Overlay Ads**: These ads appear as transparent overlay banners on the lower portion of your video. Viewers can close the ad if they choose. You earn revenue when viewers click on the ad.
4. **Display Ads**: These ads appear to the right of your video and above the video suggestions list. You earn revenue when viewers click on the ad.
5. **Sponsored Cards**: These are display ads that appear within your video as a small teaser. Viewers can click on the card to expand it and see more information. You earn revenue when viewers click on the card.

5.2.2 Enabling Ads on Your Videos

To start monetizing your videos through ads, you need to enable monetization on your YouTube channel. Follow these steps to enable ads on your videos:

1. **Sign in to YouTube Studio**: Go to the YouTube Studio website and sign in with your Google account.
2. **Click on "Monetization"**: In the left-hand menu, click on "Monetization" to access the monetization settings for your channel.
3. **Review the YouTube Partner Program terms**: Before enabling monetization, you will need to review and accept the terms of the YouTube Partner Program.
4. **Enable monetization**: Once you have reviewed the terms, click on the "Start" button to enable monetization for your channel.
5. **Set up an AdSense account**: If you don't have an AdSense account already, you will be prompted to create one during the monetization setup process. AdSense is the platform that allows you to earn revenue from ads on your videos.
6. **Link your YouTube channel to AdSense**: Follow the instructions to link your YouTube channel to your AdSense account. This step is crucial for receiving payments for your ad revenue.
7. **Enable ad formats**: After linking your AdSense account, you can choose which ad formats you want to enable on your videos. Consider the ad formats we discussed earlier and select the ones that align with your content and audience preferences.
8. **Submit your channel for review**: Once you have enabled ads on your videos, your channel will go through a review process to ensure it complies with YouTube's policies. This review process may take some time, so be patient.

5.2.3 Optimizing Ad Revenue

Enabling ads on your videos is just the first step towards monetizing your channel. To maximize your ad revenue, you need to optimize various aspects of your content and channel. Here are some strategies to help you optimize your ad revenue:

1. **Create high-quality content**: Advertisers are more likely to place ads on videos that have high production value and engage viewers. Focus on creating compelling and valuable content that keeps your audience coming back for more.
2. **Optimize video length**: Longer videos tend to generate more ad revenue, as there are more opportunities for ads to be displayed. However, it's important to strike a balance between video length and viewer engagement. Avoid unnecessarily long videos that may lead to viewer drop-off.
3. **Strategically place ads**: Experiment with different ad placements to find the optimal balance between viewer experience and revenue generation. Consider placing ads at natural breaks in your content or during moments of high viewer engagement.
4. **Monitor ad performance**: Regularly review your YouTube Analytics to gain insights into how your ads are performing. Pay attention to metrics such as ad impressions, click-through rates, and revenue generated. Use this data to make informed decisions about ad optimization.
5. **Engage with your audience**: Building a loyal and engaged audience can lead to higher ad revenue. Encourage viewers to like, comment, and share your videos, as this can increase engagement and attract more advertisers.
6. **Experiment with ad formats**: Test different ad formats to see which ones resonate best with your audience. Monitor viewer feedback and adjust your ad strategy accordingly.
7. **Stay up to date with YouTube policies**: YouTube's ad policies can change over time. Stay informed about any updates or changes to ensure your content remains compliant and eligible for monetization.

By enabling and optimizing ads on your videos, you can generate a steady stream of revenue from your YouTube channel. However, it's important to strike a balance between monetization and viewer experience. Always prioritize creating valuable and engaging content that keeps your audience coming back for more.

5.3 Exploring Alternative Revenue Streams

While the YouTube Partner Program and ad revenue are popular ways to monetize your channel, there are also alternative revenue streams that you can explore to diversify your income and maximize your earning potential. In this section, we will discuss some of these alternative revenue streams and how you can leverage them to generate additional income from your YouTube channel.

5.3.1 Affiliate Marketing

Affiliate marketing is a popular method of earning money online, and it can be a great way to monetize your YouTube channel. With affiliate marketing, you promote products or services in your videos and include special tracking links in the video description or through annotations. When viewers click on these links and make a purchase, you earn a commission.

To get started with affiliate marketing, you need to join affiliate programs that are relevant to your niche. Look for companies or brands that offer affiliate programs and sign up for them. Once approved, you will receive unique affiliate links that you can use in your videos.

When promoting affiliate products, it's important to be transparent with your audience and disclose that you may earn a commission from purchases made through your links. This builds trust with your viewers and ensures that you comply with the Federal Trade Commission's guidelines.

To effectively promote affiliate products, choose products that align with your channel's content and audience's interests. Create informative and engaging videos that highlight the benefits of the products and how they can solve your viewers' problems. Be genuine and authentic in your recommendations to build trust with your audience.

5.3.2 Sponsored Content

Another way to generate income from your YouTube channel is through sponsored content. Sponsored content involves partnering with brands or companies to create videos that promote their products or services. In exchange for featuring their products in your videos, you receive payment or other forms of compensation.

To attract sponsors, you need to build a strong and engaged audience. Brands are more likely to collaborate with YouTubers who have a significant following and high engagement rates. Focus on creating high-quality content that resonates with your audience and demonstrates your expertise in your niche.

When approaching brands for sponsorship opportunities, it's important to be professional and showcase the value you can provide. Create a media kit that includes information about your channel's demographics, engagement metrics, and previous collaborations. Reach out to brands that align with your channel's content and target audience, and pitch your ideas for sponsored videos.

When creating sponsored content, it's crucial to maintain transparency with your audience. Clearly disclose that the video is sponsored and explain the nature of the partnership. Be honest and authentic in your reviews and recommendations to maintain the trust of your viewers.

5.3.3 Merchandise and Product Sales

If you have a dedicated fan base, selling merchandise and products can be a lucrative revenue stream. You can create and sell branded merchandise such as t-shirts, hoodies, mugs, or even digital products like e-books or online courses.

To get started with merchandise sales, you can use print-on-demand services that handle the production, fulfillment, and shipping of your products. These services allow you to design your merchandise and set up an online store without the need for inventory or upfront costs.

Promote your merchandise in your videos and include links to your online store in the video description. Engage with your audience and create a sense of exclusivity by offering limited edition or personalized items. Consider running special promotions or discounts to incentivize your viewers to make a purchase.

In addition to merchandise, you can also create and sell digital products related to your niche. If you have expertise in a particular area, consider creating e-books, online courses, or exclusive content that your audience can purchase. These digital products can provide additional value to your viewers while generating income for your channel.

5.3.4 Crowdfunding

Crowdfunding platforms like Patreon and Kickstarter can be a great way to generate income from your YouTube channel while building a community of dedicated supporters. With crowdfunding, your viewers can contribute a monthly or one-time payment to support your channel and gain access to exclusive perks or content.

To successfully implement crowdfunding, you need to provide unique and valuable incentives for your supporters. Consider offering early access to videos, behind-the-scenes content, personalized shoutouts, or exclusive live streams. Engage with your supporters and make them feel like they are part of a special community.

Promote your crowdfunding campaign in your videos and include links in the video description. Clearly explain the benefits of supporting your channel and how the funds will be used to improve the quality of your content. Regularly update your supporters on the progress of your channel and show appreciation for their contributions.

5.3.5 Live Events and Workshops

If you have a strong and engaged audience, you can consider organizing live events or workshops related to your channel's content. These events can include meet-ups, workshops, conferences, or even online webinars. By charging admission or registration fees, you can generate income while providing additional value to your audience.

When planning live events, consider the logistics such as venue, date, and ticketing. Promote the event through your YouTube channel, social media platforms, and email newsletters. Create a sense of excitement and exclusivity to encourage your viewers to attend.

During the event, provide valuable content, networking opportunities, and interactive sessions. Engage with your audience and make them feel like they are part of a community. Collect feedback and testimonials from attendees to improve future events and build credibility.

By exploring these alternative revenue streams, you can diversify your income and maximize your earning potential as a YouTube creator. Remember to always prioritize the needs and interests of your audience and maintain transparency in your business partnerships. With dedication, creativity, and a strong work ethic, you can turn your YouTube channel into a sustainable and profitable venture.

5.4 Building Relationships with Sponsors and Brands

One of the most exciting aspects of becoming a YouTube sensation is the opportunity to collaborate with sponsors and brands. Building relationships with sponsors and brands can not only provide financial support for your channel but also open doors to new opportunities and expand your reach to a wider audience. In this section, we will explore the steps you can take to build strong relationships with sponsors and brands.

5.4.1 Identifying Potential Sponsors and Brands

Before you can start building relationships with sponsors and brands, it's important to identify the ones that align with your channel's niche and values. Consider the following steps to find potential sponsors and brands:

1. Research: Conduct thorough research to identify brands that are relevant to your content and target audience. Look for brands that have a similar target demographic or share similar values with your channel.
2. Analyze competitors: Study other YouTubers in your niche who have successfully collaborated with sponsors and brands. Take note of the brands they have worked with and the types of collaborations they have done.
3. Reach out to your audience: Engage with your audience through comments, social media, and live streams. Ask them about the brands they would like to see you collaborate with. This can give you valuable insights into potential sponsors and brands that your audience is interested in.
4. Attend industry events: Attend industry events, conferences, and trade shows related to your niche. These events provide an excellent opportunity to network with representatives from potential sponsors and brands.

5.4.2 Crafting a Compelling Sponsorship Proposal

Once you have identified potential sponsors and brands, it's time to craft a compelling sponsorship proposal that showcases the value you can provide to them. Here are some key elements to include in your proposal:

1. Introduction: Start by introducing yourself and your channel. Provide a brief overview of your content, target audience, and the unique value you bring to the table.
2. Alignment: Explain why you believe the sponsor or brand is a good fit for your channel. Highlight the similarities in values, target audience, or content themes.
3. Benefits: Clearly outline the benefits the sponsor or brand will receive by collaborating with you. This could include exposure to your engaged audience, increased brand awareness, product reviews, or endorsements.
4. Collaboration Ideas: Present creative and unique collaboration ideas that align with both your channel and the sponsor or brand. This could include sponsored videos, product placements, giveaways, or brand integrations.
5. Metrics and Analytics: Provide relevant metrics and analytics to showcase the growth and engagement of your channel. This will help sponsors and brands understand the potential reach and impact of collaborating with you.
6. Contact Information: Include your contact information and encourage the sponsor or brand to reach out to you for further discussion.

5.4.3 Reaching Out to Sponsors and Brands

Once you have crafted a compelling sponsorship proposal, it's time to reach out to potential sponsors and brands. Here are some tips to make a strong impression:

1. Personalize your approach: Avoid sending generic emails or messages to sponsors and brands. Take the time to research and understand their values, products, and recent campaigns. Personalize your outreach to show that you have done your homework.
2. Be professional and concise: Keep your initial outreach professional and concise. Introduce yourself, briefly explain why you are reaching out, and highlight the value you can provide. Attach your sponsorship proposal for their reference.
3. Follow up: If you don't receive a response within a reasonable timeframe, don't be discouraged. Follow up politely to remind them of your initial outreach and express your continued interest in collaborating.
4. Network and leverage connections: Utilize your network and connections to get introductions to sponsors and brands. Attend industry events and engage with representatives from potential sponsors and brands. Building relationships in person can often lead to more fruitful collaborations.

5.4.4 Nurturing Relationships with Sponsors and Brands

Building relationships with sponsors and brands is not just about securing one-time collaborations. It's about nurturing long-term partnerships that benefit both parties. Here are some tips to nurture relationships with sponsors and brands:

1. Deliver on your promises: When you collaborate with a sponsor or brand, make sure to deliver on your promises. Provide high-quality content that aligns with their expectations and meets the agreed-upon deliverables.
2. Communicate regularly: Maintain open lines of communication with sponsors and brands. Keep them updated on the progress of collaborations, share insights and analytics, and seek feedback to continuously improve.

3. Provide value beyond collaborations: Look for opportunities to provide value to sponsors and brands beyond the initial collaboration. This could include featuring their products in future videos, mentioning them in social media posts, or participating in their marketing campaigns.

4. Be professional and reliable: Always maintain a professional and reliable approach when working with sponsors and brands. Respond to emails and messages promptly, meet deadlines, and be respectful of their time and resources.

5. Seek feedback and learn from experiences: After each collaboration, seek feedback from sponsors and brands. Learn from their insights and experiences to improve future collaborations and strengthen your relationships.

Remember, building relationships with sponsors and brands takes time and effort. Be patient, persistent, and proactive in your approach. As your channel grows and your influence increases, more opportunities for collaborations will come your way.

6 Engaging Your Audience

6.1 Creating Compelling Thumbnails and Titles

One of the most important aspects of creating a successful YouTube channel is capturing the attention of potential viewers. In a sea of countless videos, your thumbnails and titles play a crucial role in attracting viewers and enticing them to click on your content. In this section, we will explore the strategies and techniques to create compelling thumbnails and titles that will help you stand out from the crowd and increase your chances of going viral.

6.1.1 Understanding the Importance of Thumbnails

Thumbnails are the small images that viewers see before clicking on a video. They serve as a visual representation of your content and can greatly impact whether or not someone decides to watch your video. A well-designed thumbnail can pique curiosity, convey the essence of your video, and entice viewers to click.

When creating thumbnails, keep the following tips in mind:

1. **Be eye-catching**: Use bright and contrasting colors, bold fonts, and high-quality images to grab attention. Avoid cluttered or confusing designs that may confuse viewers.
2. **Use relevant images**: Choose an image that accurately represents the content of your video. This will help set expectations and attract viewers who are genuinely interested in your topic.
3. **Include text**: Adding text to your thumbnail can provide additional context and entice viewers to click. Use clear and concise text that complements the image and conveys the main idea of your video.
4. **Maintain consistency**: Establishing a consistent visual style for your thumbnails can help viewers recognize your videos in their feed. This

can be achieved through consistent branding elements such as colors, fonts, and layouts.

6.1.2 Crafting Compelling Titles

Titles are equally important as thumbnails in capturing the attention of potential viewers. A well-crafted title can make your video stand out in search results and entice viewers to click. Here are some tips for creating compelling titles:

1. **Be concise and descriptive**: Keep your titles short and to the point while accurately describing the content of your video. Avoid clickbait titles that mislead viewers, as this can harm your channel's reputation.
2. **Include keywords**: Incorporate relevant keywords in your title to improve searchability. Think about the words or phrases that viewers might use when searching for content similar to yours.
3. **Create curiosity**: Spark curiosity by using intriguing or thought-provoking titles. This can compel viewers to click on your video to satisfy their curiosity.
4. **Use numbers and lists**: Titles that include numbers or lists tend to attract attention. For example, "10 Tips for…" or "5 Ways to…". This format provides a clear structure and promises specific information to viewers.
5. **Consider your target audience**: Tailor your titles to resonate with your target audience. Use language and tone that appeals to them and aligns with the overall theme of your channel.

6.1.3 Testing and Analyzing

Creating compelling thumbnails and titles is not a one-size-fits-all approach. It's essential to test different variations and analyze their performance to understand what works best for your audience. YouTube provides analytics tools that allow you to track the click-through rate (CTR) of your thumbnails and titles.

Experiment with different designs, images, and titles to see which ones generate the highest CTR. Pay attention to the feedback and engagement from your viewers to gain insights into what they find appealing. Use this data to refine your thumbnail and title creation process and continuously improve the clickability of your videos.

6.1.4 Staying Authentic and True to Your Content

While it's important to create compelling thumbnails and titles, it's equally crucial to stay authentic and true to your content. Misleading viewers with clickbait thumbnails and titles may initially attract clicks, but it can harm your channel's reputation in the long run. Building trust with your audience is essential for long-term success on YouTube.

Ensure that your thumbnails and titles accurately represent the content of your videos. This will help you attract viewers who are genuinely interested in your content and increase the likelihood of them becoming loyal subscribers.

Remember, creating compelling thumbnails and titles is just one piece of the puzzle. The quality and value of your content are equally important. Strive to create engaging and informative videos that deliver on the promises made in your thumbnails and titles. By combining captivating visuals with valuable content, you'll be on your way to becoming a YouTube sensation.

In the next section, we will explore how to utilize end screens and cards to further engage your audience and increase viewer retention.

6.2 Utilizing End Screens and Cards

Once you have created compelling thumbnails and titles for your videos, it's time to take your engagement with your audience to the next level. One effective way to do this is by utilizing end screens and cards. These features provided by YouTube allow you to promote your content, encourage viewers to take specific actions, and increase overall viewer engagement. In this section, we will explore how to effectively use end screens and cards to maximize the impact of your videos.

6.2.1 Understanding End Screens

End screens are interactive elements that appear during the last 5-20 seconds of your video. They provide an opportunity to promote your other videos, playlists, channels, or even external websites. End screens are a powerful tool to keep viewers engaged and encourage them to continue watching your content or explore more of your channel.

To utilize end screens effectively, follow these steps:

1. Access the YouTube Studio and navigate to the video you want to add an end screen to.
2. Click on the "End screen & Annotations" tab.
3. Choose the type of end screen element you want to add, such as video or playlist promotion, subscribe button, or link to an approved website.
4. Customize the end screen element by selecting the specific video, playlist, or channel you want to promote.
5. Adjust the duration and position of the end screen element on the video timeline.
6. Preview the end screen to ensure it appears as intended.
7. Save and publish your changes.

When creating end screens, keep in mind the following best practices:

- Keep the end screen visually appealing and consistent with your channel's branding.
- Use clear and concise text to convey the purpose of each end screen element.
- Prioritize the most relevant and engaging content to promote.
- Test different end screen layouts and elements to see what resonates best with your audience.

6.2.2 Leveraging Cards

Cards are another interactive feature provided by YouTube that can be used to engage viewers and promote related content. Unlike end screens, cards can be added at any point during your video and can be used to link to other videos, playlists, channels, or external websites. Cards are displayed as small, rectangular notifications that viewers can click on to access the promoted content.

To effectively leverage cards, follow these steps:

1. Access the YouTube Studio and navigate to the video you want to add cards to.
2. Click on the "Cards" tab.
3. Select the type of card you want to add, such as video or playlist promotion, channel promotion, or link to an approved website.
4. Customize the card by selecting the specific video, playlist, or channel you want to promote, or by entering the URL of the external website.
5. Adjust the timing of the card's appearance in the video.
6. Preview the card to ensure it appears as intended.
7. Save and publish your changes.

Consider the following tips when using cards:

- Use cards strategically to enhance the viewer's experience and provide additional value.

- Place cards at relevant moments in your video to capture the viewer's attention.
- Limit the number of cards used in a single video to avoid overwhelming the viewer.
- Monitor the performance of your cards through YouTube Analytics to identify which cards are most effective.

6.2.3 Best Practices for End Screens and Cards

To make the most of end screens and cards, consider the following best practices:

1. Keep the end screens and cards visually consistent with your channel's branding to maintain a cohesive look and feel.
2. Use compelling and concise text to encourage viewers to take action.
3. Place end screens and cards strategically to maximize their visibility and impact.
4. Test different end screen and card layouts to determine what resonates best with your audience.
5. Monitor the performance of your end screens and cards through YouTube Analytics to identify areas for improvement.
6. Regularly update and optimize your end screens and cards to keep your content fresh and engaging.

By effectively utilizing end screens and cards, you can enhance viewer engagement, promote your content, and encourage viewers to take specific actions. These features provide valuable opportunities to keep your audience connected to your channel and increase overall viewer satisfaction. Experiment with different layouts, elements, and strategies to find what works best for your channel and audience. Remember, the key to success on YouTube is to continuously adapt and improve your content and engagement strategies based on viewer feedback and analytics.

6.3 Encouraging Likes, Comments, and Subscriptions

One of the key factors in becoming a successful YouTube sensation is to engage with your audience and encourage them to like, comment, and subscribe to your channel. These actions not only increase your video's visibility but also help build a loyal community of viewers. In this section, we will explore effective strategies to encourage likes, comments, and subscriptions on your YouTube channel.

6.3.1 Creating Engaging Content

The first and most important step in encouraging likes, comments, and subscriptions is to create engaging and high-quality content. Your videos should be informative, entertaining, and provide value to your viewers. Here are some tips to create engaging content:

1. **Know your audience:** Understand the interests and preferences of your target audience. Tailor your content to meet their needs and expectations.
2. **Be authentic:** Be yourself and let your personality shine through your videos. Authenticity helps build a connection with your viewers and encourages them to engage with your content.
3. **Tell a story:** Incorporate storytelling techniques in your videos to captivate your audience. A compelling narrative keeps viewers engaged and encourages them to like, comment, and subscribe.
4. **Use visuals and editing techniques:** Utilize high-quality visuals, such as appealing thumbnails and well-edited videos, to grab viewers' attention. Visuals play a crucial role in encouraging engagement.
5. **Include a call to action:** At the end of each video, encourage your viewers to like, comment, and subscribe. Clearly state the benefits of doing so, such as receiving updates on new content or being part of a supportive community.

6.3.2 Engaging with Your Viewers

Engaging with your viewers is essential to building a loyal community and encouraging likes, comments, and subscriptions. Here are some strategies to effectively engage with your audience:

1. **Respond to comments:** Take the time to read and respond to comments on your videos. Show appreciation for positive feedback and address any questions or concerns. Engaging in conversations with your viewers makes them feel valued and encourages them to continue engaging with your content.
2. **Ask questions:** Encourage viewers to leave comments by asking thought-provoking questions related to your video's content. This prompts them to share their opinions and experiences, fostering a sense of community.
3. **Run contests or giveaways:** Organize contests or giveaways that require viewers to like, comment, and subscribe to enter. This not only incentivizes engagement but also helps increase your channel's visibility as viewers share the contest with others.
4. **Feature viewer comments:** Highlight interesting or insightful comments from your viewers in future videos. This not only acknowledges their contribution but also encourages others to engage with your content in hopes of being featured.

6.3.3 Optimizing Video Descriptions and Titles

Optimizing your video descriptions and titles can significantly impact your video's discoverability and encourage engagement. Here are some tips to optimize your video descriptions and titles:

1. **Use relevant keywords:** Research and include relevant keywords in your video titles and descriptions. This helps your videos appear in search results when viewers are looking for content similar to yours.

2. **Write compelling titles:** Craft attention-grabbing titles that accurately represent the content of your videos. A well-written title piques viewers' curiosity and encourages them to click on your video.
3. **Include a clear call to action:** In your video descriptions, explicitly ask viewers to like, comment, and subscribe. Remind them of the benefits they will receive by engaging with your channel.
4. **Add timestamps:** If your video contains different sections or topics, consider adding timestamps in the description. This allows viewers to navigate to specific parts of the video, increasing engagement and watch time.

6.3.4 Collaborating with Your Audience

Collaborating with your audience is an effective way to encourage likes, comments, and subscriptions. Here are some strategies to collaborate with your viewers:

1. **Create response videos:** Encourage your viewers to create response videos to your content. This not only fosters engagement but also helps expand your reach as their audience discovers your channel.
2. **Feature viewer content:** Showcase viewer-generated content in your videos. This could include fan art, testimonials, or video clips related to your content. By featuring your viewers' work, you make them feel appreciated and encourage others to engage with your channel.
3. **Host live Q&A sessions:** Schedule live Q&A sessions where viewers can ask you questions in real-time. This interactive format encourages engagement and allows you to connect with your audience on a personal level.
4. **Create polls and surveys:** Use the community tab on your YouTube channel to create polls and surveys. This allows your viewers to actively participate and provide feedback, making them feel involved in the content creation process.

By implementing these strategies, you can effectively encourage likes, comments, and subscriptions on your YouTube channel. Remember, building a loyal and engaged audience takes time and consistent effort. Stay dedicated to creating valuable content and engaging with your viewers, and you'll be on your way to becoming a YouTube sensation.

6.4 Responding to Feedback and Criticism

As a YouTube creator, it's important to understand that feedback and criticism are inevitable. While positive feedback can boost your confidence and motivate you to continue creating content, negative feedback and criticism can be challenging to handle. However, learning how to respond to feedback and criticism in a constructive and professional manner is crucial for your growth as a YouTube sensation. In this section, we will explore effective strategies for responding to feedback and criticism on YouTube.

6.4.1 Embrace Constructive Feedback

Constructive feedback is valuable for your growth as a YouTube creator. It provides insights into areas where you can improve and helps you understand your audience's preferences better. When receiving constructive feedback, it's important to approach it with an open mind and a willingness to learn. Instead of taking it personally, view it as an opportunity to enhance your content and engage with your audience on a deeper level.

To effectively embrace constructive feedback:

1. Stay calm and composed: It's natural to feel defensive when receiving criticism, but it's important to remain calm and composed. Take a deep breath and remind yourself that feedback is meant to help you improve.
2. Analyze the feedback objectively: Take the time to analyze the feedback objectively. Consider the validity of the points raised and evaluate whether they align with your goals and vision for your channel.
3. Separate emotions from the feedback: It's easy to let emotions cloud your judgment when receiving feedback. Try to separate your emotions from the feedback and focus on the constructive aspects.

4. Appreciate the feedback: Show gratitude to those who take the time to provide feedback. Let them know that you value their input and that it will help you improve your content.
5. Take action: Once you've analyzed the feedback, take appropriate action to address the areas of improvement. Implement changes in your content, video quality, or any other aspect that the feedback highlights.

6.4.2 Handling Negative Comments

Negative comments are an unfortunate reality of being a YouTube creator. While it can be disheartening to receive negative comments, it's important to handle them in a professional and respectful manner. Here are some strategies for effectively dealing with negative comments:

1. Don't take it personally: Remember that negative comments are not a reflection of your worth as a creator. People have different opinions, and it's impossible to please everyone. Don't let negative comments discourage you or affect your self-esteem.
2. Evaluate the comment's validity: Not all negative comments are constructive. Some may be rude or irrelevant. Evaluate the comment's validity and consider whether it provides any valuable insights or suggestions for improvement.
3. Respond with empathy and professionalism: When responding to negative comments, maintain a professional and empathetic tone. Avoid getting defensive or engaging in arguments. Instead, try to understand the commenter's perspective and respond in a respectful manner.
4. Ignore trolls and abusive comments: Some comments may be purely intended to provoke or insult. It's best to ignore such comments and not engage with trolls. Focus your energy on engaging with constructive feedback and fostering a positive community on your channel.
5. Use negative comments as an opportunity for growth: Negative comments can be a source of motivation to improve your content. Use

them as an opportunity to learn and grow as a creator. Remember, even the most successful YouTubers receive negative comments, so you're not alone in this experience.

6.4.3 Engaging with Criticism

Criticism, whether constructive or not, can be challenging to handle. However, engaging with criticism in a positive and productive manner can help you build a stronger connection with your audience. Here are some tips for effectively engaging with criticism:

1. Respond promptly: When you receive criticism, try to respond promptly. This shows that you value your audience's opinions and are open to dialogue.
2. Acknowledge the criticism: Start by acknowledging the criticism and thanking the person for taking the time to provide their feedback. This demonstrates your willingness to listen and engage with your audience.
3. Seek clarification: If the criticism is unclear or vague, politely ask for clarification. This will help you better understand the commenter's perspective and address their concerns more effectively.
4. Provide explanations or solutions: If the criticism is valid, provide explanations or solutions to address the issue. This shows that you take feedback seriously and are committed to improving your content.
5. Encourage further discussion: Engage in a constructive conversation with the commenter and encourage further discussion. This can help you gain valuable insights and foster a sense of community on your channel.

Remember, not all criticism requires a response. Use your judgment to determine which comments warrant engagement and which can be addressed indirectly through improvements in your content.

6.4.4 Learning from Feedback

Feedback, whether positive or negative, is an opportunity for growth and improvement. By actively listening to your audience and learning from their feedback, you can refine your content and enhance your YouTube presence. Here are some ways to effectively learn from feedback:

1. Identify patterns: Look for recurring themes or patterns in the feedback you receive. This can help you identify areas where you consistently excel or areas that need improvement.
2. Experiment and iterate: Use feedback as a guide to experiment with new ideas and approaches. Implement changes in your content, video structure, or presentation style based on the feedback you receive.
3. Monitor audience response: Pay attention to how your audience responds to the changes you make based on feedback. Analyze metrics such as likes, comments, and view duration to gauge the impact of your improvements.
4. Continuously seek feedback: Actively seek feedback from your audience through comments, surveys, or polls. Regularly ask for their opinions and suggestions to ensure you stay connected with their needs and preferences.
5. Stay true to your vision: While feedback is valuable, it's important to stay true to your creative vision. Use feedback as a tool to refine your content, but don't compromise your unique style or authenticity in the process.

By embracing feedback and criticism, you can foster a stronger connection with your audience, improve your content, and continue growing as a YouTube sensation. Remember, feedback is an essential part of the creative process, and by responding to it with professionalism and openness, you can turn it into a catalyst for success.

7 Promoting Your Videos

7.1 Optimizing Video Titles, Descriptions, and Tags

One of the key factors in getting your YouTube videos discovered by a wider audience is optimizing your video titles, descriptions, and tags. These elements play a crucial role in helping YouTube's algorithm understand what your video is about and who it might be relevant to. By optimizing these components, you can increase the chances of your videos appearing in search results and recommended video sections. In this section, we will explore some strategies to optimize your video titles, descriptions, and tags to maximize your video's visibility and reach.

7.1.1 Crafting Effective Video Titles

The video title is the first thing viewers see when they come across your video, so it's essential to make it compelling and attention-grabbing. Here are some tips for crafting effective video titles:

1. Be concise and descriptive: Keep your titles short and to the point while accurately reflecting the content of your video. Avoid clickbait titles that mislead viewers.
2. Use keywords: Incorporate relevant keywords in your video titles to improve searchability. Think about what words or phrases your target audience might use when searching for content like yours.
3. Create curiosity: Engage viewers by piquing their curiosity with intriguing titles. Pose a question, offer a solution, or promise valuable information to entice them to click on your video.
4. Include numbers and statistics: Numbers in titles tend to attract attention and suggest that the video offers specific information or tips. For example, "10 Ways to Boost Your Productivity" or "5 Secrets to Perfecting Your Makeup."
5. Test and analyze: Experiment with different title formats and analyze the performance of your videos. Pay attention to which titles generate

more clicks and engagement, and use that information to refine your future titles.

7.1.2 Writing Compelling Video Descriptions

Video descriptions provide an opportunity to provide additional context and information about your video. Here are some tips for writing compelling video descriptions:

1. Start with a hook: Begin your description with a captivating sentence that summarizes the main point or value of your video. This will encourage viewers to continue reading and watching.
2. Include relevant keywords: Incorporate relevant keywords naturally throughout your description to improve search visibility. However, avoid keyword stuffing, as it can negatively impact your video's ranking.
3. Provide a summary: Give a brief overview of what viewers can expect from your video. Highlight the main topics or key takeaways to entice viewers to watch.
4. Add timestamps: If your video covers multiple topics or sections, consider adding timestamps in the description. This allows viewers to navigate directly to the sections they are most interested in.
5. Include links and calls to action: Use the description to promote your other videos, playlists, social media channels, or website. You can also encourage viewers to like, comment, and subscribe to your channel.
6. Engage with your audience: Invite viewers to leave comments or ask questions in the description. Responding to comments can help foster a sense of community and encourage more engagement.

7.1.3 Optimizing Video Tags

Tags are keywords or phrases that help YouTube understand the content of your video. They play a crucial role in determining where your video appears in search results and related video suggestions. Here are some tips for optimizing your video tags:

1. Use relevant and specific tags: Choose tags that accurately describe the content of your video. Be specific rather than using broad terms. For example, instead of using "food," use "healthy recipes for breakfast."
2. Include variations and synonyms: Add variations and synonyms of your main tags to capture a wider range of search queries. This can help your video appear in more search results.
3. Research popular tags: Look for popular tags related to your video's topic by analyzing the tags used by successful videos in your niche. Tools like YouTube's search suggestions and third-party keyword research tools can be helpful in finding relevant tags.
4. Avoid irrelevant tags: Don't include tags that are unrelated to your video's content. This can lead to a negative user experience and may harm your video's visibility.
5. Update tags over time: As your channel and content evolve, revisit your video tags periodically to ensure they remain relevant and aligned with your current content.

Remember, optimizing your video titles, descriptions, and tags is an ongoing process. Continuously monitor the performance of your videos and make adjustments as needed. By implementing these strategies, you can increase the visibility of your videos and attract a larger audience to your YouTube channel.

7.2 Sharing Videos on Social Media Platforms

Once you have created and optimized your YouTube videos, it's time to share them on social media platforms to reach a wider audience and increase your chances of going viral. Social media platforms provide a great opportunity to promote your videos and engage with your viewers on a more personal level. In this section, we will explore some effective strategies for sharing your videos on social media platforms.

7.2.1 Choosing the Right Social Media Platforms

Before you start sharing your videos on social media, it's important to identify the platforms that are most relevant to your target audience. Different social media platforms have different demographics and user behaviors, so it's crucial to choose the ones that align with your content and goals. Here are some popular social media platforms you can consider:

1. **Facebook**: With over 2.8 billion monthly active users, Facebook is a great platform to share your videos and engage with your audience. You can create a Facebook page for your YouTube channel and share your videos directly on your page. Additionally, you can join relevant Facebook groups and communities to connect with like-minded individuals and share your videos there.

2. **Twitter**: Twitter is a fast-paced platform where you can share short and engaging snippets of your videos. You can create tweets with catchy captions, GIFs, or images to grab the attention of your followers. Utilize relevant hashtags and tag influencers or brands that are related to your content to increase your reach.

3. **Instagram**: Instagram is a visually-driven platform that allows you to share images and short videos. You can create eye-catching thumbnails or snippets from your videos and share them on your

Instagram feed or stories. Utilize relevant hashtags and engage with your followers through comments and direct messages.

4. **LinkedIn**: If your content is more professional or educational in nature, LinkedIn can be a great platform to share your videos. You can create LinkedIn articles or posts that provide valuable insights related to your videos and include a link to your YouTube channel. Engage with professionals in your industry and join relevant LinkedIn groups to expand your network.

5. **Pinterest**: Pinterest is a platform where users discover and save ideas for various topics. You can create visually appealing pins that represent your videos and link them back to your YouTube channel. Utilize relevant keywords and descriptions to optimize your pins for search.

6. **TikTok**: TikTok is a short-form video platform that has gained immense popularity in recent years. You can create engaging and entertaining snippets from your videos and share them on TikTok. Utilize popular trends and challenges to increase your visibility and reach a younger audience.

Remember, it's not necessary to be present on all social media platforms. Choose the ones that align with your content and target audience, and focus on building a strong presence there.

7.2.2 Creating Engaging Social Media Posts

Once you have chosen the social media platforms you want to focus on, it's time to create engaging posts that will attract viewers to your YouTube videos. Here are some tips for creating compelling social media posts:

1. **Use eye-catching visuals**: Include captivating images, thumbnails, or short video snippets that grab the attention of your audience. Visuals play a crucial role in enticing users to click on your videos.

2. **Write compelling captions**: Craft catchy and concise captions that highlight the key points or benefits of watching your video. Use persuasive language and include relevant hashtags to increase discoverability.

3. **Include a call-to-action**: Encourage your audience to take action by including a clear call-to-action in your social media posts. Ask them to like, comment, share, or subscribe to your YouTube channel.
4. **Leverage trending topics**: Stay updated with the latest trends and incorporate them into your social media posts. This can help you ride the wave of popular conversations and increase your chances of going viral.
5. **Engage with your audience**: Respond to comments, messages, and mentions on social media platforms. Engaging with your audience shows that you value their feedback and builds a loyal community around your channel.

7.2.3 Scheduling and Consistency

Consistency is key when it comes to sharing your videos on social media platforms. Create a schedule for posting your videos and stick to it. This will help you build anticipation among your audience and establish a routine for them to engage with your content. Utilize social media management tools like Hootsuite or Buffer to schedule your posts in advance and save time.

Additionally, analyze the performance of your social media posts using the analytics provided by each platform. This will help you understand which types of posts resonate the most with your audience and optimize your future content accordingly.

7.2.4 Engaging with Your Social Media Community

Building a community around your YouTube channel is crucial for long-term success. Engage with your social media community by responding to comments, messages, and mentions. Show appreciation for their support and encourage them to share your videos with their own networks. This will help you build a loyal and active community that will continue to support and promote your content.

Remember, social media platforms are not just a one-way street. Engage with other content creators, influencers, and brands in your niche. Collaborate with them, share their content, and build mutually beneficial relationships. This will not only help you expand your reach but also establish yourself as an active and supportive member of the community.

In the next section, we will explore how to utilize YouTube's community features to further promote your videos and engage with your audience.

7.3 Utilizing YouTube's Community Features

YouTube is not just a platform for uploading and sharing videos; it is also a vibrant community of creators and viewers. To truly become a YouTube sensation, you need to tap into the power of this community and engage with your audience. In this section, we will explore the various community features that YouTube offers and how you can utilize them to promote your videos and build a loyal fan base.

7.3.1 Interacting with Your Subscribers

One of the most important aspects of building a successful YouTube channel is establishing a strong connection with your subscribers. YouTube provides several features that allow you to interact with your audience and foster a sense of community. Here are some ways you can engage with your subscribers:

1. Responding to Comments

Take the time to read and respond to comments on your videos. This shows your viewers that you value their feedback and encourages them to continue engaging with your content. Reply to both positive and negative comments in a respectful and genuine manner.

2. Hosting Live Q&A Sessions

YouTube Live allows you to host live streams where you can interact with your audience in real-time. Consider hosting Q&A sessions where your subscribers can ask you questions and receive immediate responses. This not only strengthens your relationship with your audience but also provides valuable content for your channel.

3. Creating Community Posts

YouTube's Community tab allows you to create posts that appear in your subscribers' feeds. Use this feature to share updates, behind-the-scenes content, or ask for feedback and suggestions. Engaging with your subscribers through Community posts helps to keep them connected and invested in your channel.

7.3.2 Collaborating with Other YouTubers

Collaborating with other YouTubers is a powerful way to expand your reach and tap into new audiences. YouTube provides several features that make collaboration easier and more effective. Here's how you can leverage these features:

1. Featured Channels

YouTube allows you to feature other channels on your own channel page. This is a great way to promote your collaborations and introduce your audience to other creators they might enjoy. Reach out to other YouTubers in your niche and propose featuring each other's channels to cross-promote your content.

2. Collaborative Videos

Creating videos with other YouTubers not only provides fresh and exciting content for your audience but also exposes you to their subscribers. Plan and execute collaborative projects that align with both of your audiences' interests. This can be in the form of interviews, challenges, or even joint series.

3. Cross-Promotion

In addition to featuring channels, you can also cross-promote each other's videos within your own content. Mention and link to your collaborator's videos in your own videos, and encourage them to do the same. This helps to drive traffic between your channels and exposes your content to new viewers.

7.3.3 Participating in YouTube Communities

YouTube Communities are groups of creators and viewers who share common interests. By actively participating in these communities, you can connect with like-minded individuals and gain exposure for your channel. Here's how you can make the most of YouTube Communities:

1. Joining Relevant Communities

Search for and join communities that align with your niche or content. Engage with other members by commenting on their posts, sharing your expertise, and providing valuable insights. This not only helps you establish yourself as an authority but also exposes your channel to potential new viewers.

2. Sharing Your Content

Once you have established a presence in relevant communities, you can share your own videos with the community members. However, it's important to do this in a non-spammy and genuine way. Share your videos when they are relevant to the discussion and provide value to the community.

3. Collaborating within Communities

YouTube Communities also provide opportunities for collaboration. Look for creators within the community who have complementary content or skills and propose collaboration projects. This can be in the form of guest appearances, joint videos, or even community-wide events.

7.3.4 Engaging with Online Communities and Forums

In addition to YouTube's own community features, there are numerous online communities and forums where creators and viewers gather to discuss various topics. Engaging with these communities can help you expand your reach and connect with potential viewers. Here's how you can effectively engage with online communities:

1. Find Relevant Communities and Forums

Research and identify online communities and forums that are relevant to your niche or target audience. Look for platforms such as Reddit, Quora, or specialized forums where discussions related to your content are taking place.

2. Provide Value and Expertise

When engaging with online communities, focus on providing value and showcasing your expertise. Answer questions, share insights, and participate in discussions in a helpful and meaningful way. This establishes you as a knowledgeable and trustworthy creator, encouraging others to check out your channel.

3. Avoid Self-Promotion

While it's important to share your content, it's equally important to avoid excessive self-promotion. Instead of simply dropping links to your videos, focus on building relationships and contributing to the community. When appropriate, share your videos as a valuable resource that can help answer specific questions or provide further information.

By utilizing YouTube's community features and engaging with online communities, you can expand your reach, build a loyal fan base, and increase the chances of your videos going viral. Remember, building a successful YouTube channel is not just about creating great content; it's also about fostering a sense of community and connecting with your audience.

7.4 Engaging with Online Communities and Forums

Engaging with online communities and forums is a powerful strategy to promote your YouTube videos and grow your channel. These platforms provide an opportunity to connect with like-minded individuals, share your content, and gain valuable feedback. By actively participating in these communities, you can increase your visibility, attract new viewers, and build a loyal audience. In this section, we will explore the steps you can take to effectively engage with online communities and forums.

7.4.1 Identify Relevant Communities and Forums

The first step in engaging with online communities and forums is to identify the platforms that are relevant to your niche. Conduct thorough research to find communities and forums where your target audience is active. Look for platforms that have a large user base and high engagement levels. Consider both general platforms and those specific to your niche. For example, if you create cooking videos, you may want to join cooking forums or food-related communities.

7.4.2 Understand the Rules and Guidelines

Before actively participating in any online community or forum, it is crucial to familiarize yourself with the rules and guidelines of each platform. Each community may have its own set of rules regarding self-promotion, content sharing, and engagement. Make sure to read and understand these guidelines to avoid any potential issues or conflicts. Adhering to the rules will help you establish a positive reputation within the community and build trust with other members.

7.4.3 Contribute Valuable Content

Once you have identified the relevant communities and forums, it's time to start contributing valuable content. Remember, the key to successful engagement is to provide value to the community rather than solely promoting your own content. Share your expertise, answer questions, and provide helpful insights. By consistently contributing valuable content, you will establish yourself as a trusted and respected member of the community.

7.4.4 Share Your YouTube Videos Strategically

While it's important to contribute valuable content, you can also strategically share your YouTube videos within the community. However, make sure to follow the platform's guidelines regarding self-promotion. Instead of simply dropping a link to your video, provide context and explain why the video is relevant to the community. This approach will increase the chances of other members watching and engaging with your content.

7.4.5 Engage with Other Community Members

Engagement is a two-way street. To build meaningful connections within online communities and forums, it's essential to engage with other members. Take the time to read and comment on other people's posts, provide feedback, and participate in discussions. By actively engaging with others, you will not only establish yourself as a valuable member but also increase the likelihood of others reciprocating and engaging with your content.

7.4.6 Seek Feedback and Advice

Online communities and forums are excellent platforms to seek feedback and advice from fellow creators and viewers. Share your videos and ask for constructive criticism. Be open to feedback and use it to improve the quality of your content. Additionally, you can ask for advice on specific topics related to YouTube growth, video editing, or content creation. The insights and suggestions you receive can be invaluable in your journey to becoming a YouTube sensation.

7.4.7 Be Respectful and Professional

When engaging with online communities and forums, it's crucial to maintain a respectful and professional demeanor. Treat others with kindness and respect, even if you encounter differing opinions or negative feedback. Avoid engaging in arguments or heated debates. Remember, your behavior within these communities reflects not only on your personal brand but also on your YouTube channel. Building a positive reputation will help you attract more viewers and potential collaborators.

7.4.8 Monitor and Respond to Comments

In addition to engaging with online communities and forums, it's equally important to monitor and respond to comments on your YouTube videos. Responding to comments shows your viewers that you value their feedback and appreciate their engagement. Take the time to reply to comments, answer questions, and acknowledge positive feedback. This level of interaction will foster a sense of community and encourage viewers to continue engaging with your content.

7.4.9 Track Your Progress and Adjust Strategies

As you engage with online communities and forums, it's essential to track your progress and evaluate the effectiveness of your strategies. Monitor the engagement levels on your YouTube videos and analyze the traffic coming from these platforms. Keep track of the communities and forums that generate the most engagement and focus your efforts on those platforms. Additionally, be open to adjusting your strategies based on the feedback and insights you receive from the community.

7.4.10 Network and Collaborate

Engaging with online communities and forums can also open doors for networking and collaboration opportunities. As you build relationships with fellow creators and viewers, explore the possibility of collaborating on projects or cross-promoting each other's channels. Collaborations can introduce your content to a new audience and help you grow your subscriber base. Networking within these communities can also lead to potential sponsorships or brand partnerships in the future.

By actively engaging with online communities and forums, you can expand your reach, attract new viewers, and establish yourself as a YouTube sensation. Remember to contribute valuable content, strategically share your videos, engage with other community members, and maintain a respectful and professional demeanor. With consistent effort and genuine interaction, you can leverage these platforms to accelerate your YouTube success.

8 Collaborating with Other YouTubers

8.1 Finding and Approaching Potential Collaborators

Collaborating with other YouTubers can be a great way to expand your audience, increase your reach, and create unique and engaging content. By teaming up with like-minded creators, you can tap into their existing fan base and introduce your channel to a whole new audience. In this section, we will explore how to find and approach potential collaborators for your YouTube channel.

8.1.1 Identifying Potential Collaborators

The first step in finding potential collaborators is to identify creators who align with your niche and target audience. Look for channels that have a similar content style, theme, or audience demographic as yours. This will ensure that your collaboration is relevant and appealing to both your audiences.

Start by researching popular channels in your niche. Look for creators who have a similar number of subscribers or slightly more. This will increase the likelihood of them being open to collaboration. Take note of their content, engagement levels, and overall brand image.

Additionally, pay attention to the engagement of their audience. Look for channels with active and engaged viewers who regularly comment, like, and share their videos. This indicates that the creator has built a loyal and dedicated community, which can be beneficial for your collaboration.

8.1.2 Utilizing YouTube's Search and Recommendations

YouTube provides several tools and features that can help you find potential collaborators. One of the most effective ways is to use the search bar and enter relevant keywords related to your niche. This will generate a list of channels and videos that are popular in your niche.

You can also explore the "Related Channels" section on the right-hand side of a video page. This feature suggests channels that are similar to the one you are currently watching. It's a great way to discover creators who share a similar audience and content style.

Another useful tool is YouTube's recommendations. Pay attention to the videos that YouTube suggests to you based on your viewing history and preferences. This can lead you to channels that you may not have discovered otherwise.

8.1.3 Engaging with Potential Collaborators

Once you have identified potential collaborators, it's time to engage with them. Start by subscribing to their channel and watching their videos. Leave thoughtful and genuine comments on their videos to show your support and appreciation for their content. This will help you establish a connection and make them more likely to consider collaborating with you.

Additionally, engage with their community by responding to comments left by their viewers. This will not only showcase your engagement but also give you an opportunity to interact with their audience and potentially attract new subscribers to your channel.

8.1.4 Reaching Out and Pitching Collaboration Ideas

After establishing a connection with potential collaborators, it's time to reach out and pitch your collaboration ideas. Start by sending them a personalized message through YouTube's messaging system or through their social media platforms. Be polite, concise, and professional in your approach.

In your message, introduce yourself and your channel, highlighting why you believe a collaboration would be beneficial for both parties. Be specific about the type of collaboration you have in mind, whether it's a joint video, a series, or a guest appearance. Explain how your collaboration can provide value to their audience and vice versa.

It's important to be flexible and open to their suggestions as well. Collaborations work best when both parties have a shared vision and are willing to compromise and adapt their ideas. Be prepared to discuss potential video topics, filming logistics, and promotion strategies.

8.1.5 Building Long-Term Collaborative Relationships

Collaborations shouldn't be seen as one-off opportunities but as a way to build long-term relationships with other creators. Once you have successfully collaborated with someone, continue to support their channel by sharing their content, leaving comments, and engaging with their audience.

Consider creating a series or recurring collaborations with the same creators. This will not only provide consistency for your audience but also strengthen your relationship with your collaborators. By working together on multiple projects, you can develop a deeper understanding of each other's content and create a synergy that benefits both channels.

Remember, collaboration is a two-way street. Be generous with your support and promotion of your collaborators' content. This will encourage them to reciprocate and help promote your channel to their audience as well.

In conclusion, finding and approaching potential collaborators requires research, engagement, and effective communication. By identifying creators in your niche, engaging with their content, and pitching collaboration ideas, you can build valuable partnerships that will benefit both your channel and your audience. Collaborations not only expand your reach but also provide an opportunity for creative growth and learning from other successful creators.

8.2 Planning and Executing Collaborative Projects

Collaborating with other YouTubers can be a powerful strategy to grow your channel and reach a wider audience. By working together with like-minded creators, you can create engaging and unique content that benefits both parties involved. In this section, we will explore the process of planning and executing collaborative projects on YouTube.

8.2.1 Identifying Potential Collaborators

The first step in planning a collaborative project is to identify potential collaborators who align with your channel's niche and target audience. Look for creators who have a similar style, content theme, or audience demographic. You can find potential collaborators by:

1. Researching: Spend time exploring YouTube and other social media platforms to find creators who share similar interests or content themes. Look for channels that have a similar number of subscribers or engagement levels to ensure a balanced collaboration.
2. Engaging with the Community: Participate in online communities, forums, and social media groups related to your niche. Engage with other creators and build relationships by commenting on their videos, sharing their content, and offering support. This can help you establish connections and find potential collaborators.
3. Networking at Events: Attend industry events, conferences, and meetups where you can meet other creators in person. These events provide an excellent opportunity to network, exchange ideas, and discuss potential collaboration projects.

8.2.2 Brainstorming Collaborative Ideas

Once you have identified potential collaborators, it's time to brainstorm ideas for your collaborative project. Consider the following factors when brainstorming:

1. Common Interests: Find common interests or topics that both you and your collaborator are passionate about. This will ensure that the project is engaging and authentic for both parties.
2. Unique Angle: Look for a unique angle or approach that sets your collaborative project apart from others. This could be a new format, a different perspective, or a creative twist that captures the attention of your audience.
3. Complementary Skills: Consider the skills and expertise of your collaborator. Look for ways to leverage each other's strengths to create a well-rounded and high-quality project.
4. Audience Appeal: Keep your target audience in mind when brainstorming ideas. Ensure that the collaborative project will resonate with your audience and provide value to them.

8.2.3 Planning the Collaboration

Once you have a solid idea for your collaborative project, it's time to plan the details. Here are some steps to consider:

1. Define Roles and Responsibilities: Clearly define the roles and responsibilities of each collaborator. Determine who will be responsible for scripting, filming, editing, and promoting the collaborative project.
2. Set Deadlines: Establish a timeline for the project, including deadlines for scriptwriting, filming, editing, and release. Setting deadlines will help keep everyone accountable and ensure the project stays on track.
3. Communication and Coordination: Establish effective communication channels with your collaborator(s). Use tools like email, messaging

apps, or project management platforms to stay in touch and coordinate the project's progress.

4. Scripting and Storyboarding: Collaboratively develop a script and storyboard for the project. This will help ensure that both parties are aligned on the content and structure of the video.

5. Equipment and Resources: Determine what equipment and resources are needed for the project. Coordinate with your collaborator(s) to ensure that everyone has access to the necessary tools and resources.

8.2.4 Executing the Collaboration

With the planning phase complete, it's time to execute the collaborative project. Here are some tips to make the execution process smooth and successful:

1. Filming: Coordinate with your collaborator(s) to schedule the filming sessions. Ensure that everyone is prepared with the necessary equipment and props. Communicate clearly about the shooting locations, timings, and any specific requirements.

2. Collaboration Dynamics: Maintain open communication and a positive working relationship with your collaborator(s). Be open to feedback, suggestions, and compromises to create a harmonious collaboration experience.

3. Editing and Post-Production: Once the filming is complete, work together to edit and finalize the video. Share the editing responsibilities or consider hiring a professional editor to ensure a polished final product.

4. Promotion and Release: Coordinate the promotion and release of the collaborative project. Plan a joint marketing strategy, including sharing the video on both channels, promoting it on social media, and engaging with your audiences to generate excitement.

8.2.5 Evaluating the Collaboration

After the collaborative project is released, take the time to evaluate its success and impact. Consider the following aspects:

1. Audience Response: Monitor the comments, likes, and shares on the collaborative video. Pay attention to the engagement levels and feedback from your audience to gauge their response.
2. Analytics and Metrics: Analyze the performance of the collaborative video using YouTube Analytics. Look at metrics like views, watch time, audience retention, and subscriber growth to assess the impact of the collaboration.
3. Feedback and Reflection: Seek feedback from your collaborator(s) and reflect on the collaboration experience. Identify what worked well and areas for improvement to enhance future collaborations.

By planning and executing collaborative projects effectively, you can leverage the strengths of other creators, expand your audience reach, and create exciting content that resonates with your viewers. Collaboration not only benefits your channel but also fosters a sense of community within the YouTube ecosystem. So, start reaching out to potential collaborators and embark on exciting collaborative projects to take your channel to new heights.

8.3 Cross-Promoting Each Other's Channels

Collaborating with other YouTubers can be a powerful strategy to grow your channel and reach a wider audience. By cross-promoting each other's channels, you can tap into each other's existing fan base and gain exposure to new viewers who may be interested in your content. In this section, we will explore effective ways to cross-promote each other's channels and maximize the benefits of collaboration.

8.3.1 Finding Compatible YouTubers

The first step in cross-promoting each other's channels is to find compatible YouTubers who share a similar target audience or niche. Look for creators who produce content that complements your own and aligns with your brand. This will ensure that the collaboration feels natural and resonates with both your audiences.

To find compatible YouTubers, you can:

1. Research within your niche: Explore other channels within your niche and identify creators who have a similar style or content theme. Pay attention to their subscriber count, engagement rate, and overall channel growth.
2. Utilize YouTube's search and recommendation features: Use relevant keywords and filters to search for channels that match your niche. YouTube's recommendation algorithm can also suggest similar channels based on your viewing history.
3. Engage with your audience: Pay attention to the comments section of your videos and social media platforms. Look for viewers who mention other YouTubers or express interest in collaborations. This can give you valuable insights into potential collaborators.

8.3.2 Approaching Potential Collaborators

Once you have identified compatible YouTubers, it's time to approach them with your collaboration proposal. Keep in mind that successful collaborations are built on mutual benefit and shared goals. When reaching out to potential collaborators, consider the following tips:

1. Personalize your message: Take the time to research the creator's content and mention specific videos or aspects that you enjoyed. This shows that you have taken a genuine interest in their work.
2. Highlight the benefits: Clearly communicate the benefits of collaborating with you. Explain how cross-promotion can help both channels grow, reach new audiences, and provide value to viewers.
3. Propose a collaboration idea: Present a specific collaboration idea that aligns with both your channels. This could be a joint video, a series of videos, or even a live stream event. Make sure the idea is compelling and showcases the strengths of both channels.
4. Be professional and respectful: Maintain a professional tone in your communication and respect the other creator's time and boundaries. Understand that not all creators may be available or interested in collaborating, and that's okay.

8.3.3 Planning and Executing Cross-Promotion

Once you have found compatible YouTubers and received positive responses, it's time to plan and execute the cross-promotion. Here are some steps to follow:

1. Define the collaboration goals: Clearly define the goals and objectives of the collaboration. This could include increasing subscribers, boosting views, or expanding reach. Having a shared understanding of the desired outcomes will help guide the collaboration process.
2. Plan the content: Collaborate with the other YouTuber to plan the content for the cross-promotion. Brainstorm ideas, create a script or

outline, and decide on the format and structure of the collaboration. Ensure that the content is engaging, valuable, and aligns with both channels' branding.

3. Coordinate release schedules: Coordinate with the other YouTuber to determine the release schedule for the cross-promotion. Ideally, both channels should release the collaboration video or content simultaneously or within a short timeframe to maximize the impact.

4. Cross-promote on your channels: Once the collaboration content is ready, promote it on your channel. Create a teaser or trailer to generate excitement and anticipation among your subscribers. Include links to the other YouTuber's channel and encourage your viewers to check out their content.

5. Engage with the audience: During and after the cross-promotion, actively engage with the audience on both channels. Respond to comments, answer questions, and show appreciation for the support. This will help foster a sense of community and encourage viewers to explore both channels further.

8.3.4 Maximizing the Benefits of Cross-Promotion

To maximize the benefits of cross-promotion, consider the following strategies:

1. Collaborate regularly: Building long-term collaborative relationships can be highly beneficial for both channels. Consider collaborating with the same YouTubers on multiple occasions to create a sense of familiarity and continuity for your audience.

2. Share resources and expertise: Cross-promotion is not just about promoting each other's channels; it's also an opportunity to share resources and expertise. Exchange tips, strategies, and insights with your collaborators to help each other grow and improve.

3. Leverage social media: In addition to promoting the collaboration on your YouTube channel, leverage social media platforms to amplify the reach. Share behind-the-scenes content, teasers, and updates on

platforms like Instagram, Twitter, and Facebook to generate buzz and attract new viewers.

4. Collaborate with influencers: Consider collaborating with influencers or celebrities who have a significant following. Their endorsement and promotion can greatly boost the visibility and credibility of your channel.

Remember, cross-promotion is a two-way street. Be sure to reciprocate the support and promote your collaborator's channel on your own platform. By working together, you can both benefit from increased exposure, new subscribers, and a stronger presence in the YouTube community.

In the next section, we will explore how to build long-term collaborative relationships and foster a supportive network of YouTubers.

8.4 Building Long-Term Collaborative Relationships

Collaborating with other YouTubers can be a powerful way to grow your channel and reach a wider audience. By working together, you can leverage each other's strengths, share resources, and create content that is more engaging and valuable to your viewers. Building long-term collaborative relationships is essential for sustained success on YouTube. In this section, we will explore strategies to foster strong partnerships and maintain fruitful collaborations.

8.4.1 Finding the Right Collaborators

When it comes to collaborating with other YouTubers, it's important to find creators who align with your channel's niche, values, and target audience. Look for creators who have a similar style, content format, or topic as yours. This will ensure that your collaborations are authentic and resonate with both your audiences.

To find potential collaborators, you can start by researching popular channels in your niche. Look for creators who have a similar subscriber count or engagement level as yours. This will help ensure that the collaboration is mutually beneficial and that you can provide value to each other's audiences.

You can also join online communities and forums dedicated to YouTube creators. These platforms often have sections where creators can connect and collaborate. Engaging with other creators in these communities can help you find like-minded individuals who are interested in collaborating.

8.4.2 Approaching Potential Collaborators

Once you have identified potential collaborators, it's time to reach out to them. When approaching other YouTubers for collaboration, it's important to be professional, respectful, and genuine. Here are some tips for making a good impression:

1. Personalize your message: Take the time to research the creator's content and mention specific videos or aspects that you enjoyed. This shows that you have taken an interest in their work and increases the chances of getting a positive response.
2. Be clear about your intentions: Clearly communicate why you think a collaboration would be beneficial for both parties. Highlight how your audiences can benefit from the collaboration and what unique value you can bring to the table.
3. Offer a mutually beneficial idea: Propose a collaboration idea that aligns with both your and the other creator's content. Make sure the idea is exciting, engaging, and has the potential to attract a wider audience.
4. Be flexible and open to suggestions: Collaboration is a two-way street, so be open to suggestions and modifications to the initial idea. This will help foster a sense of teamwork and ensure that both parties are invested in the project.

8.4.3 Planning and Executing Collaborative Projects

Once you have found a collaborator and agreed on a collaboration idea, it's time to plan and execute the project. Here are some steps to ensure a smooth collaboration process:

1. Set clear goals and expectations: Discuss and agree upon the goals, objectives, and expectations for the collaboration. This includes the type of content, format, timeline, and any specific deliverables.
2. Divide responsibilities: Clearly define each collaborator's role and responsibilities. This will help avoid confusion and ensure that everyone knows what they need to contribute to the project.
3. Establish effective communication channels: Determine the best way to communicate and share updates throughout the collaboration. This

could be through email, messaging apps, or project management tools. Regular communication is key to keeping the project on track.

4. Create a timeline and schedule: Develop a timeline that outlines the key milestones and deadlines for the collaboration. This will help you stay organized and ensure that the project progresses smoothly.

5. Collaborate on content creation: Work together to brainstorm ideas, script the content, and plan the production process. Make sure to leverage each other's strengths and expertise to create high-quality and engaging content.

6. Coordinate promotion efforts: Discuss how you will promote the collaboration on both channels. This could include sharing teasers, cross-promoting videos, or creating joint promotional materials. By coordinating your promotion efforts, you can maximize the reach and impact of the collaboration.

8.4.4 Nurturing Long-Term Collaborative Relationships

Building long-term collaborative relationships requires ongoing effort and nurturing. Here are some strategies to maintain strong partnerships:

1. Show appreciation: Regularly express gratitude and appreciation for your collaborator's contributions. Recognize their efforts and publicly acknowledge their work. This will help foster a positive and supportive relationship.

2. Collaborate on multiple projects: Look for opportunities to collaborate on multiple projects over time. This not only strengthens the bond between you and your collaborator but also provides your audience with consistent and valuable content.

3. Support each other's channels: Continuously support each other's channels by engaging with their content, leaving comments, and sharing their videos. This helps boost each other's visibility and encourages mutual growth.

4. Attend industry events together: Whenever possible, attend industry events, conferences, or meetups together. This allows you to network,

learn from other creators, and strengthen your collaborative relationship in person.

5. Share resources and knowledge: Be open to sharing resources, tips, and insights with your collaborator. This can include equipment recommendations, editing techniques, or strategies for growing your channel. By sharing knowledge, you both can benefit and improve your content creation skills.

Remember, building long-term collaborative relationships takes time and effort. It's important to approach collaborations with a genuine desire to create valuable content and support each other's growth. By fostering strong partnerships, you can expand your reach, engage new audiences, and create content that resonates with viewers.

9 Dealing with Challenges and Setbacks

9.1 Overcoming Creative Blocks

Creating content consistently can be a challenging task, especially when you're trying to become a YouTube sensation. One of the biggest hurdles that many creators face is dealing with creative blocks. These blocks can hinder your ability to come up with fresh and engaging ideas for your videos, leading to a decline in your channel's growth and success. However, with the right strategies and mindset, you can overcome these creative blocks and continue to produce high-quality content that resonates with your audience. In this section, we will explore some effective techniques to help you overcome creative blocks and keep your creative juices flowing.

9.1.1 Embrace Inspiration from Various Sources

When you find yourself stuck in a creative rut, it's essential to seek inspiration from different sources. Explore various forms of media, such as books, movies, music, and art, to spark new ideas and perspectives. Engaging with different types of content can help you think outside the box and bring fresh concepts to your videos. Additionally, consider attending industry events, conferences, or workshops related to your niche. These events can expose you to new trends, technologies, and ideas that can inspire your content creation process.

9.1.2 Collaborate with Others

Collaboration is a powerful tool for overcoming creative blocks. Working with other YouTubers or creative individuals can bring new energy and ideas to your content. Brainstorming sessions with like-minded creators can help you generate innovative concepts and overcome any mental roadblocks you may be facing. Collaborations can also introduce you to new audiences and expand your reach. Reach out to creators in your niche or complementary niches and propose collaboration ideas that align with both of your channels' themes and goals.

9.1.3 Take Breaks and Practice Self-Care

Sometimes, creative blocks occur due to mental and physical exhaustion. It's crucial to take breaks and practice self-care to recharge your creative energy. Engage in activities that relax and rejuvenate you, such as exercising, meditating, spending time in nature, or pursuing hobbies outside of YouTube. Taking breaks allows your mind to rest and reset, enabling you to approach your content creation process with a fresh perspective. Remember, self-care is not a luxury but a necessity for maintaining your creativity and overall well-being.

9.1.4 Experiment with Different Formats and Styles

If you find yourself stuck in a creative rut, it may be helpful to experiment with different video formats and styles. Trying something new can reignite your passion for content creation and inspire fresh ideas. For example, if you typically create vlogs, consider trying out tutorials, challenges, or storytelling videos. Experimenting with different formats not only keeps your content diverse but also allows you to tap into new creative avenues and engage with your audience in unique ways.

9.1.5 Engage with Your Audience

Your audience can be a valuable source of inspiration and ideas. Interacting with your viewers through comments, social media, or live streams can provide insights into their interests, preferences, and questions. Pay attention to the feedback and suggestions they provide, as they can spark new ideas for your content. Additionally, consider conducting polls or surveys to gather direct feedback from your audience. Engaging with your viewers not only helps you overcome creative blocks but also strengthens the connection between you and your audience.

9.1.6 Create a Content Calendar and Set Realistic Goals

Having a content calendar and setting realistic goals can help you stay organized and motivated, even when facing creative blocks. Plan your video topics and upload schedule in advance, allowing yourself enough time to brainstorm and develop ideas. Breaking down your goals into smaller, achievable tasks can make the content creation process less overwhelming. By having a clear roadmap, you can focus on one step at a time and maintain consistency in your content creation, even during challenging times.

9.1.7 Seek Feedback and Critique

Feedback and constructive criticism can be invaluable in overcoming creative blocks. Share your work with trusted friends, fellow creators, or online communities and ask for their honest opinions. Their feedback can provide fresh perspectives and highlight areas for improvement. Embrace feedback as an opportunity for growth and learning, rather than taking it personally. By incorporating feedback into your content creation process, you can refine your ideas and enhance the quality of your videos.

9.1.8 Practice Mindfulness and Visualization Techniques

Mindfulness and visualization techniques can help you overcome creative blocks by quieting your mind and allowing new ideas to flow. Take a few moments each day to practice mindfulness exercises, such as deep breathing or meditation, to clear your mind of distractions and focus on the present moment. Visualization techniques involve mentally picturing yourself successfully overcoming creative blocks and producing engaging content. By visualizing positive outcomes, you can boost your confidence and stimulate your creativity.

9.1.9 Keep a Journal or Idea Bank

Maintaining a journal or idea bank can be a helpful practice for overcoming creative blocks. Whenever you come across interesting concepts, thoughts, or inspirations, jot them down in your journal or save them in a digital idea bank. This way, when you're struggling to come up with ideas, you can refer back to your collection for inspiration. Additionally, consider dedicating specific brainstorming sessions where you can freely explore and expand upon the ideas in your journal.

9.1.10 Stay Persistent and Embrace Failure

Overcoming creative blocks requires persistence and a willingness to embrace failure. Understand that creative blocks are a natural part of the creative process, and everyone experiences them at some point. Instead of getting discouraged, view creative blocks as opportunities for growth and learning. Embrace the challenges and setbacks as stepping stones towards becoming a better content creator. Remember, success often comes after multiple failures, so stay persistent and keep pushing forward.

By implementing these strategies and maintaining a positive mindset, you can overcome creative blocks and continue to produce engaging and successful content on YouTube. Remember, creativity is a journey, and it's essential to enjoy the process while striving for improvement.

9.2 Handling Negative Comments and Trolls

As a YouTube creator, it's inevitable that you will encounter negative comments and trolls at some point in your journey. While it can be disheartening and frustrating, it's important to develop strategies to handle these challenges effectively. In this section, we will explore some practical tips on how to handle negative comments and trolls on your YouTube channel.

9.2.1 Understanding Negative Comments and Trolls

Negative comments and trolls are individuals who leave derogatory, offensive, or hurtful remarks on your videos or channel. They may criticize your content, appearance, or even attack you personally. It's crucial to understand that negative comments and trolls are often seeking attention or trying to provoke a reaction. They may have different motivations, such as jealousy, boredom, or simply a desire to spread negativity.

9.2.2 Developing a Positive Mindset

When faced with negative comments and trolls, it's essential to maintain a positive mindset. Remember that not everyone will appreciate or enjoy your content, and that's okay. Focus on the positive feedback and support you receive from your audience. Surround yourself with a supportive community of fellow creators who can offer advice and encouragement during challenging times.

9.2.3 Don't Take it Personally

One of the most important things to remember when dealing with negative comments and trolls is not to take it personally. Understand that these comments are often a reflection of the commenter's own issues and insecurities, rather than a true reflection of your worth or talent as a creator.

Remind yourself that you are creating content because you are passionate about it, and not everyone will resonate with your style or message.

9.2.4 Evaluate the Validity

While it's essential not to take negative comments personally, it can still be valuable to evaluate the validity of the criticism. Some negative comments may contain constructive feedback that can help you improve your content. Take a step back and objectively assess whether there is any truth to the criticism. If there is, use it as an opportunity for growth and improvement.

9.2.5 Engage with Constructive Criticism

When you come across constructive criticism, it's important to engage with it in a positive and professional manner. Respond to the comment with gratitude for their feedback and let them know that you appreciate their perspective. Use this as an opportunity to have a meaningful conversation and show your audience that you value their input. By engaging with constructive criticism, you can foster a sense of community and build stronger relationships with your viewers.

9.2.6 Ignore and Delete

Not all negative comments and trolls warrant a response. In fact, engaging with trolls can often fuel their behavior and give them the attention they seek. If a comment is clearly meant to provoke or spread negativity without any constructive value, it's best to ignore and delete it. By removing these comments from your channel, you create a more positive and welcoming environment for your audience.

9.2.7 Use Moderation Tools

YouTube provides various moderation tools that can help you manage negative comments and trolls effectively. Familiarize yourself with these tools and utilize them to your advantage. You can enable comment filters to automatically hide or review comments that contain specific keywords or phrases. Additionally, you can block specific users from commenting on your videos or channel altogether. These tools give you more control over the type of content and interactions you allow on your channel.

9.2.8 Seek Support from Your Community

When dealing with negative comments and trolls, it's crucial to lean on your community for support. Reach out to fellow creators, friends, or family members who can offer guidance and encouragement. Share your experiences with others who have faced similar challenges and learn from their strategies for handling negativity. Remember, you are not alone in this journey, and there are people who understand and can provide the support you need.

9.2.9 Report and Flag Inappropriate Comments

If you come across comments that are offensive, hateful, or violate YouTube's community guidelines, it's important to report and flag them. YouTube takes these violations seriously and will take appropriate action against users who engage in such behavior. By reporting inappropriate comments, you contribute to creating a safer and more positive environment for yourself and your audience.

9.2.10 Focus on the Positive

Lastly, it's crucial to focus on the positive aspects of your YouTube journey. Remember why you started creating content in the first place and the impact you have on your audience. Celebrate the positive feedback, engagement, and growth you experience. By shifting your focus to the positive aspects of your channel, you can maintain your motivation and continue creating content that resonates with your audience.

Handling negative comments and trolls is an inevitable part of being a YouTube creator. By developing a positive mindset, evaluating the validity of criticism, engaging with constructive feedback, and utilizing moderation tools, you can effectively manage these challenges. Remember to seek support from your community, report inappropriate comments, and focus on the positive aspects of your YouTube journey. Stay resilient, and don't let negativity deter you from pursuing your passion as a YouTube sensation.

9.3 Managing Time and Burnout

Creating and maintaining a successful YouTube channel requires a significant investment of time and energy. As you work towards becoming a YouTube sensation, it's crucial to manage your time effectively and avoid burnout. In this section, we will explore strategies to help you balance your workload, maintain your motivation, and prevent exhaustion.

9.3.1 Prioritize and Plan Your Tasks

One of the most effective ways to manage your time as a YouTube creator is to prioritize and plan your tasks. Start by creating a to-do list or using a project management tool to organize your responsibilities. Break down your tasks into smaller, manageable chunks and assign deadlines to each of them.

When prioritizing your tasks, consider the importance and urgency of each item. Focus on completing high-priority tasks first, ensuring that you allocate enough time for content creation, editing, and engaging with your audience. By having a clear plan in place, you can stay on track and avoid feeling overwhelmed.

9.3.2 Set Realistic Goals and Deadlines

Setting realistic goals and deadlines is essential for managing your time effectively. While it's important to challenge yourself, it's equally important to be realistic about what you can achieve within a given timeframe. Set specific, measurable, achievable, relevant, and time-bound (SMART) goals that align with your overall vision for your YouTube channel.

Break down your long-term goals into smaller milestones and assign deadlines to each of them. This will help you stay focused and motivated as you work towards achieving your objectives. Remember to be flexible and adjust your goals and deadlines as needed, taking into account any unexpected challenges or changes in your circumstances.

9.3.3 Create a Schedule and Stick to It

Establishing a consistent schedule is crucial for managing your time effectively as a YouTube creator. Determine the best times for content creation, editing, and engaging with your audience, and allocate specific time slots for each activity. This will help you maintain a sense of structure and ensure that you dedicate enough time to each aspect of your channel.

Consider your personal preferences and energy levels when creating your schedule. Some creators find it helpful to work during their most productive hours, while others prefer to tackle challenging tasks when they have fewer distractions. Experiment with different schedules until you find a routine that works best for you, and make a commitment to stick to it.

9.3.4 Delegate and Outsource Tasks

As your YouTube channel grows, you may find it challenging to handle all aspects of your channel on your own. Consider delegating or outsourcing certain tasks to lighten your workload and prevent burnout. For example, you could hire an editor to help with video editing or a virtual assistant to manage your social media accounts.

When delegating tasks, ensure that you provide clear instructions and expectations to the individuals you are working with. Regularly communicate and provide feedback to ensure that the work is being done to your satisfaction. By offloading some responsibilities, you can focus on the aspects of your channel that require your unique skills and expertise.

9.3.5 Take Breaks and Practice Self-Care

While it's important to work hard and stay committed to your YouTube channel, it's equally important to take breaks and practice self-care. Pushing yourself too hard without allowing for rest and relaxation can lead to burnout and a decline in the quality of your content.

Schedule regular breaks throughout your day to recharge and rejuvenate. Engage in activities that help you relax and unwind, such as exercising, meditating, or spending time with loved ones. Prioritize getting enough sleep and maintaining a healthy lifestyle, as these factors can significantly impact your energy levels and overall well-being.

9.3.6 Seek Support and Accountability

Building a successful YouTube channel can be a challenging journey, and it's essential to seek support and accountability along the way. Connect with other YouTubers who understand the unique challenges you face and can provide guidance and encouragement. Join online communities or attend YouTube creator meetups to network and learn from others in the industry.

Consider finding an accountability partner or joining a mastermind group where you can regularly check in with others and hold each other accountable for your goals. Having a support system can help you stay motivated, share ideas, and navigate through any challenges or setbacks you may encounter.

9.3.7 Recognize and Manage Burnout

Despite your best efforts, there may be times when you experience burnout. It's crucial to recognize the signs and take proactive steps to manage it. Some common signs of burnout include feeling exhausted, lacking motivation, experiencing decreased creativity, and feeling overwhelmed by your responsibilities.

If you notice these signs, take a step back and reassess your workload and priorities. Consider taking a short break from creating content or reducing your posting frequency temporarily. Use this time to recharge, reflect, and rediscover your passion for creating content. Seek support from your community and consider consulting with a mental health professional if needed.

Remember, managing time and preventing burnout is an ongoing process. Continuously evaluate and adjust your strategies as your channel grows and your circumstances change. By prioritizing your well-being and effectively managing your time, you can maintain your motivation, create high-quality content, and continue on your path to becoming a YouTube sensation.

9.4 Adapting to YouTube Algorithm Changes

As a YouTube creator, it is essential to stay up-to-date with the ever-evolving YouTube algorithm. The algorithm determines which videos are recommended to users, impacting your channel's visibility and growth. Adapting to these changes is crucial for maintaining and increasing your success on the platform. In this section, we will explore strategies to adapt to YouTube algorithm changes effectively.

9.4.1 Understanding the YouTube Algorithm

Before diving into adapting to algorithm changes, it is crucial to understand how the YouTube algorithm works. The algorithm considers various factors when recommending videos to users, including:

1. **Watch Time**: The total amount of time viewers spend watching your videos.
2. **Engagement**: The number of likes, comments, shares, and subscribers your videos receive.
3. **Click-Through Rate (CTR)**: The percentage of users who click on your video after seeing it in their recommendations or search results.
4. **Video Retention**: How long viewers watch your videos before leaving.
5. **Relevance**: How well your video matches a user's search query or interests.

By understanding these factors, you can optimize your content and channel to align with the algorithm's preferences.

9.4.2 Staying Informed

YouTube algorithm changes occur regularly, and it is crucial to stay informed about these updates. YouTube often releases official statements or blog posts regarding algorithm changes, providing insights into what creators should focus on. Additionally, following YouTube creators and industry experts who discuss algorithm updates can help you stay ahead of the curve.

9.4.3 Analyzing Your Analytics

Regularly analyzing your YouTube analytics is essential for understanding how algorithm changes impact your channel. Pay close attention to metrics such as watch time, engagement, CTR, and video retention. By identifying patterns and trends, you can determine how algorithm changes affect your channel's performance.

9.4.4 Experimenting with Content

Adapting to algorithm changes often requires experimenting with different types of content. The algorithm may favor specific formats or topics at different times. By diversifying your content and trying new ideas, you can increase your chances of aligning with the algorithm's preferences. Monitor the performance of your videos and identify which types of content resonate best with your audience and the algorithm.

9.4.5 Optimizing Video Metadata

Video metadata plays a crucial role in helping the algorithm understand and categorize your content. Optimize your video titles, descriptions, and tags to include relevant keywords that align with your target audience's interests. However, avoid keyword stuffing and ensure that your metadata accurately represents the content of your videos.

9.4.6 Consistency and Regular Uploads

Consistency is key when it comes to adapting to algorithm changes. The algorithm tends to favor channels that consistently upload high-quality content. Develop a regular upload schedule and stick to it. This not only helps you build an engaged audience but also signals to the algorithm that your channel is active and reliable.

9.4.7 Engaging with Your Audience

Engagement is a crucial factor in the YouTube algorithm. Encourage your viewers to like, comment, and share your videos. Respond to comments and foster a sense of community on your channel. The more engagement your videos receive, the more likely they are to be recommended by the algorithm.

9.4.8 Collaborating with Other Creators

Collaborating with other creators can help increase your channel's visibility and reach. When you collaborate with other creators, you tap into their audience, exposing your content to new viewers. This increased exposure can positively impact your channel's performance and help you adapt to algorithm changes.

9.4.9 Monitoring Trends and User Behavior

Staying on top of current trends and understanding user behavior is essential for adapting to algorithm changes. Monitor popular topics and formats within your niche and create content that aligns with these trends. Additionally, pay attention to your audience's preferences and adapt your content accordingly.

9.4.10 Seeking Feedback and Iterating

Adapting to algorithm changes requires a willingness to seek feedback and iterate on your content. Pay attention to the comments and feedback you receive from your viewers. Use this feedback to improve your videos and align them with the algorithm's preferences. Continuously iterate and refine your content strategy based on the insights you gather.

9.4.11 Patience and Persistence

Adapting to algorithm changes takes time and patience. It is essential to remember that not every video will perform exceptionally well. Stay persistent and continue creating high-quality content that resonates with your audience.

Over time, as you adapt to algorithm changes and refine your content strategy, you will see the results you desire.

By following these strategies and staying adaptable, you can effectively navigate and adapt to YouTube algorithm changes. Remember, the algorithm is designed to showcase the best content to users, so focus on creating valuable and engaging videos that resonate with your audience.

10 Expanding Your YouTube Presence

10.1 Creating a Website or Blog for Your Channel

In today's digital age, having a strong online presence is crucial for success as a YouTube creator. While YouTube provides a platform for sharing your videos and engaging with your audience, creating a website or blog can further enhance your brand and expand your reach. In this section, we will explore the benefits of having a website or blog for your YouTube channel and provide a step-by-step guide on how to create one.

10.1.1 Why Create a Website or Blog?

Having a website or blog dedicated to your YouTube channel offers several advantages that can help you grow your audience and establish your brand. Here are some key benefits:

1. **Centralized Hub:** A website or blog serves as a centralized hub for all your content. It allows you to showcase your videos, provide additional information about yourself and your channel, and offer resources and exclusive content to your audience.
2. **Increased Discoverability:** By optimizing your website or blog for search engines, you can attract new viewers who may not have discovered your YouTube channel otherwise. It provides an additional avenue for people to find your content and engage with your brand.
3. **Brand Building:** A website or blog allows you to create a cohesive brand identity by customizing the design, layout, and content to align with your channel's theme. It helps you establish credibility and professionalism, making it easier to attract sponsors and collaborate with other creators.
4. **Monetization Opportunities:** With a website or blog, you can explore additional monetization opportunities beyond YouTube's Partner Program. You can display ads, promote affiliate products, sell merchandise, or offer premium content to generate revenue.

5. **Direct Communication:** Having a website or blog enables direct communication with your audience. You can engage with your viewers through comments, forums, or even a dedicated email newsletter. This direct interaction fosters a sense of community and loyalty among your audience.

10.1.2 Step-by-Step Guide to Creating a Website or Blog

Now that you understand the benefits of having a website or blog for your YouTube channel, let's dive into the step-by-step process of creating one:

Step 1: Choose a Platform

There are several platforms available for creating websites or blogs, each with its own set of features and customization options. Some popular options include WordPress, Wix, Squarespace, and Blogger. Research each platform and choose the one that best suits your needs in terms of design flexibility, ease of use, and cost.

Step 2: Select a Domain Name

A domain name is the web address that people will use to access your website or blog. Choose a domain name that reflects your channel's brand and is easy to remember. Ideally, it should be the same or similar to your YouTube channel name. Check the availability of your desired domain name and register it through a domain registrar.

Step 3: Set Up Hosting

Hosting is the service that allows your website or blog to be accessible on the internet. Select a hosting provider that offers reliable service, good customer support, and affordable pricing. Many website builders offer hosting as part of their packages, simplifying the process.

Step 4: Customize the Design

Once you have chosen a platform, domain name, and hosting, it's time to customize the design of your website or blog. Select a theme or template that aligns with your channel's branding and customize it to your liking. Add your logo, choose a color scheme, and organize the layout to create a visually appealing and user-friendly website.

Step 5: Create Pages and Sections

Create pages and sections on your website or blog to showcase your content and provide additional information to your audience. Some essential pages to include are:

- **Home:** A welcoming page that introduces your channel and highlights your best content.
- **About:** A page that provides information about yourself, your channel's mission, and your journey as a creator.
- **Videos:** A page where you can embed your YouTube videos or create playlists for easy navigation.
- **Blog:** If you choose to have a blog, create a dedicated page where you can share written content related to your channel's niche.
- **Contact:** A page that allows viewers to get in touch with you, whether through a contact form or your social media handles.

Step 6: Optimize for SEO

To increase the discoverability of your website or blog, optimize it for search engines. Research relevant keywords related to your channel's niche and incorporate them into your page titles, headings, and content. Write compelling meta descriptions and alt tags for your images. Regularly update your website with fresh and engaging content to improve its search engine ranking.

Step 7: Integrate with Your YouTube Channel

To create a seamless experience for your audience, integrate your website or blog with your YouTube channel. Add links to your channel and social media profiles on your website's header or footer. Embed your YouTube videos on relevant pages to encourage viewers to explore your channel further. Cross-promote your website on your YouTube videos and descriptions to drive traffic.

Step 8: Engage with Your Audience

Once your website or blog is up and running, make sure to engage with your audience. Respond to comments and messages promptly, create a forum or community section where viewers can interact with each other, and consider starting an email newsletter to keep your audience updated on new content and exclusive offers.

By following these steps and consistently updating your website or blog with valuable content, you can create a strong online presence that complements your YouTube channel and helps you become a YouTube sensation.

Remember, building a website or blog takes time and effort, so be patient and stay consistent with your content creation and promotion strategies.

10.2 Utilizing Other Video Platforms

While YouTube is undoubtedly the most popular video-sharing platform, there are other video platforms that can help you expand your reach and grow your audience. By utilizing these platforms strategically, you can increase your visibility, attract new viewers, and ultimately drive more traffic to your YouTube channel. In this section, we will explore some of the top video platforms you can leverage to expand your YouTube presence.

10.2.1 Vimeo

Vimeo is a well-known video-sharing platform that caters to a more artistic and professional audience. It is often used by filmmakers, artists, and creative professionals to showcase their work. While Vimeo has a smaller user base compared to YouTube, it offers a more curated and high-quality viewing experience.

To utilize Vimeo effectively, consider the following strategies:

1. **Cross-promote your YouTube content**: Upload teasers or previews of your YouTube videos on Vimeo to generate interest and drive traffic to your channel. Include a call-to-action in the video description or end screen to encourage viewers to watch the full video on YouTube.
2. **Engage with the Vimeo community**: Participate in Vimeo groups, forums, and discussions related to your niche. Share your expertise, provide valuable insights, and connect with like-minded creators. This can help you establish yourself as an authority in your niche and attract new viewers to your YouTube channel.
3. **Optimize your video descriptions and tags**: Just like on YouTube, optimizing your video descriptions and tags on Vimeo can improve your discoverability. Use relevant keywords, add a compelling

description, and include links to your YouTube channel and other social media platforms.

10.2.2 Dailymotion

Dailymotion is another popular video-sharing platform that attracts millions of viewers worldwide. It offers a diverse range of content, including music, sports, news, and entertainment. While Dailymotion may not have the same level of reach as YouTube, it can still be a valuable platform to promote your YouTube channel.

Here are some ways to utilize Dailymotion effectively:

1. **Repurpose your YouTube content**: Upload selected videos or highlights from your YouTube channel to Dailymotion. This allows you to reach a different audience and potentially attract new viewers who may not be active on YouTube.
2. **Leverage Dailymotion's partnerships**: Dailymotion has partnerships with various media outlets and publishers. If you have high-quality, original content, you may have the opportunity to collaborate with these partners and gain additional exposure for your YouTube channel.
3. **Engage with the Dailymotion community**: Interact with viewers, respond to comments, and participate in discussions on Dailymotion. Building relationships with the community can help you establish a loyal following and drive traffic to your YouTube channel.

10.2.3 Facebook Video

Facebook is not just a social networking platform; it has also become a significant player in the video-sharing space. With billions of active users, Facebook offers a massive potential audience for your YouTube channel.

Consider the following strategies to utilize Facebook Video effectively:

1. **Upload native videos**: Instead of simply sharing YouTube links on Facebook, upload your videos directly to the platform. Native videos tend to perform better on Facebook's algorithm and receive higher engagement.
2. **Leverage Facebook groups**: Join relevant Facebook groups in your niche and share your YouTube videos with the community. Make sure to follow the group's guidelines and engage with other members' content as well. This can help you build relationships, gain exposure, and attract new viewers to your YouTube channel.
3. **Utilize Facebook Live**: Facebook Live allows you to stream live videos to your audience. Consider hosting Q&A sessions, behind-the-scenes footage, or exclusive content on Facebook Live to engage with your viewers and promote your YouTube channel.

10.2.4 Instagram IGTV

Instagram's IGTV is a dedicated platform for long-form vertical videos. With its user-friendly interface and integration with the Instagram app, IGTV provides an excellent opportunity to reach a younger and highly engaged audience.

To utilize IGTV effectively, consider the following strategies:

1. **Create exclusive content**: Produce unique and engaging videos specifically for IGTV. This can include behind-the-scenes footage, tutorials, interviews, or vlogs that complement your YouTube content. By offering exclusive content on IGTV, you can entice viewers to follow your YouTube channel for more.
2. **Promote your YouTube videos**: Use IGTV to create teasers or previews of your YouTube videos. Include a call-to-action in the video description or comments section, directing viewers to watch the full video on your YouTube channel.
3. **Leverage Instagram's features**: Take advantage of Instagram's features, such as Stories and IGTV previews in your feed, to promote

your IGTV content. Engage with your Instagram followers, respond to comments, and use relevant hashtags to increase discoverability.

By utilizing these alternative video platforms strategically, you can expand your YouTube presence, attract new viewers, and ultimately increase your chances of becoming a YouTube sensation. Remember to tailor your content to each platform's unique audience and features, and always provide clear calls-to-action to drive traffic back to your YouTube channel.

10.3 Exploring Live Streaming and Podcasting

In today's digital landscape, content creators are constantly looking for new ways to engage with their audience and expand their reach. Two popular avenues for achieving this are live streaming and podcasting. These platforms offer unique opportunities to connect with your viewers and listeners in real-time, fostering a deeper sense of community and interaction. In this section, we will explore the benefits of live streaming and podcasting, as well as provide practical tips on how to get started.

10.3.1 Live Streaming

Live streaming has gained immense popularity in recent years, allowing creators to broadcast their content in real-time to a global audience. Whether you want to host live Q&A sessions, gaming sessions, or even showcase behind-the-scenes footage, live streaming offers a dynamic and interactive way to engage with your viewers. Here are some key benefits of incorporating live streaming into your YouTube strategy:

Building a Stronger Connection with Your Audience

Live streaming allows you to interact with your audience in real-time, fostering a sense of community and building a stronger connection. Viewers can ask questions, provide feedback, and engage with you directly, creating a more personal and intimate experience. This level of interaction can help you build a loyal fan base and establish yourself as an authority in your niche.

Creating a Sense of Urgency and Exclusivity

One of the main advantages of live streaming is the sense of urgency and exclusivity it creates. By announcing a specific date and time for your live stream, you can generate excitement and anticipation among your audience. This can lead to increased viewership and engagement, as viewers don't want to miss out on the live experience.

Repurposing Content and Expanding Reach

Live streams can be recorded and saved as videos on your channel, allowing viewers who missed the live event to watch it later. This not only gives your content a longer lifespan but also expands your reach to those who may not have been available during the live stream. Additionally, you can repurpose highlights from your live streams into shorter videos, creating additional content for your channel.

Monetization Opportunities

Live streaming opens up new monetization opportunities for creators. YouTube's Super Chat feature allows viewers to purchase and send messages during live streams, providing a way for creators to earn revenue in real-time. Additionally, you can explore sponsorships, brand collaborations, and even affiliate marketing during your live streams.

Getting Started with Live Streaming

Now that you understand the benefits of live streaming, let's explore how to get started:

1. Ensure a Stable Internet Connection

Live streaming requires a stable and reliable internet connection. Before you begin, make sure you have a strong internet connection that can handle the bandwidth required for live streaming. Consider using a wired connection for optimal stability.

2. Choose the Right Equipment

Invest in quality equipment to ensure a smooth live streaming experience. This includes a good camera, microphone, and lighting setup. Depending on your content, you may also need additional equipment such as a gaming capture card or a green screen.

3. Select a Live Streaming Platform

YouTube offers its own live streaming feature called YouTube Live. To start live streaming on YouTube, you need to verify your channel and enable live streaming in your YouTube Studio settings. Alternatively, you can explore other live streaming platforms such as Twitch or Facebook Live, depending on your target audience and content niche.

4. Plan and Promote Your Live Stream

Create a schedule for your live streams and promote them in advance to generate interest and maximize viewership. Utilize your social media channels, email newsletters, and YouTube community tab to spread the word about your upcoming live stream. Consider creating eye-catching graphics or trailers to grab your audience's attention.

5. Engage with Your Audience

During your live stream, actively engage with your audience by responding to comments, answering questions, and acknowledging viewers. This interaction is what sets live streaming apart from pre-recorded content, so make sure to prioritize engagement and create a welcoming and inclusive environment.

10.3.2 Podcasting

Podcasting has become a popular medium for content creators to share their expertise, stories, and conversations with a dedicated audience. With the rise of smartphones and on-demand audio, podcasting offers a convenient and accessible way for listeners to consume content while multitasking. Here are some reasons why you should consider podcasting:

Building a Loyal and Engaged Audience

Podcasts allow you to connect with your audience on a deeper level. Listeners often develop a sense of loyalty and trust towards podcast hosts, as they become a part of their daily routines. By consistently delivering valuable and entertaining content, you can build a dedicated and engaged audience.

Expanding Your Reach and Discoverability

Podcasting opens up new avenues for reaching a wider audience. Platforms like Apple Podcasts, Spotify, and Google Podcasts have millions of active users searching for new shows to listen to. By optimizing your podcast for search and promoting it across various channels, you can increase your discoverability and attract new listeners.

Repurposing Content and Cross-Promotion

Podcasts offer the opportunity to repurpose your existing content or create new content specifically for the audio format. You can convert blog posts, YouTube videos, or even live stream recordings into podcast episodes, giving your audience another way to consume your content. Additionally, you can cross-promote your podcast on your YouTube channel, social media platforms, and website to drive traffic and engagement.

Monetization and Sponsorship Opportunities

Similar to YouTube, podcasting offers various monetization opportunities. You can monetize your podcast through sponsorships, advertisements, or even by offering premium content or merchandise to your listeners. As your podcast grows in popularity, you may attract sponsors and brands interested in reaching your audience.

Getting Started with Podcasting

If you're ready to dive into podcasting, here are some steps to help you get started:

1. Define Your Podcast's Format and Niche

Decide on the format and niche of your podcast. Will it be an interview-style show, a solo monologue, or a combination of both? Determine the topics you want to cover and the target audience you want to reach. This will help you create focused and engaging content.

2. Choose the Right Equipment

Invest in a good quality microphone and headphones to ensure clear audio for your podcast. You may also need a pop filter, microphone stand, and audio editing software to enhance the sound quality. Test your equipment before recording to ensure everything is working properly.

3. Plan and Outline Your Episodes

Create a content plan and outline for each episode. This will help you stay organized and ensure a smooth flow of conversation or information. Consider scripting or bullet-pointing key talking points to keep the conversation on track.

4. Record and Edit Your Episodes

Find a quiet and acoustically treated space to record your podcast episodes. Use audio editing software to remove background noise, enhance audio quality, and add any necessary music or sound effects. Aim for a consistent audio level throughout the episode.

5. Choose a Podcast Hosting Platform

Select a podcast hosting platform to upload and distribute your episodes. Popular hosting platforms include Libsyn, Podbean, and Anchor. These platforms provide an RSS feed that you can submit to podcast directories like Apple Podcasts, Spotify, and Google Podcasts.

6. Promote Your Podcast

Promote your podcast across various channels to attract listeners. Utilize your existing audience on YouTube, social media, and email newsletters to spread the word about your podcast. Consider collaborating with other podcasters or appearing as a guest on other shows to expand your reach.

Conclusion

Live streaming and podcasting offer exciting opportunities to engage with your audience in real-time and expand your content reach. By incorporating these platforms into your YouTube strategy, you can create a more interactive and immersive experience for your viewers and listeners. Remember to plan, promote, and engage with your audience to make the most out of live streaming and podcasting.

10.4 Expanding Your Brand Beyond YouTube

While YouTube is undoubtedly the go-to platform for video content creators, it's important to remember that there are other avenues to explore when it comes to expanding your brand and reaching a wider audience. In this section, we will discuss various strategies and platforms that can help you take your YouTube presence to the next level.

10.4.1 Creating a Website or Blog for Your Channel

One effective way to expand your brand beyond YouTube is by creating a dedicated website or blog for your channel. This allows you to have a centralized hub where viewers can find more information about you, your content, and any other projects you may be working on. Here are some steps to get started:

1. Choose a domain name: Select a domain name that reflects your brand and is easy for viewers to remember. Consider using your channel name or a variation of it.
2. Set up hosting: Find a reliable hosting provider and set up your website. There are many options available, so do some research to find the one that best suits your needs.
3. Design your website: Create a visually appealing and user-friendly website that aligns with your channel's branding. Include sections such as an about page, contact information, and links to your social media accounts.
4. Publish content: Regularly update your website with blog posts, behind-the-scenes content, and updates about upcoming projects. This will keep your audience engaged and encourage them to visit your website regularly.
5. Optimize for search engines: Implement search engine optimization (SEO) techniques to improve your website's visibility in search

engine results. Use relevant keywords, meta tags, and descriptive titles to attract organic traffic.

6. Promote your website: Share links to your website on your YouTube channel, social media platforms, and other online communities. Encourage your viewers to visit your website for exclusive content and updates.

10.4.2 Utilizing Other Video Platforms

While YouTube is the dominant video-sharing platform, there are other platforms that can help you expand your brand and reach a different audience. Here are a few popular alternatives:

1. Vimeo: Known for its high-quality video playback, Vimeo is a great platform for showcasing your creative work. Consider uploading exclusive content or behind-the-scenes footage to engage with a different audience.
2. Dailymotion: With a large international user base, Dailymotion can help you reach viewers from around the world. Explore uploading your videos to this platform to expand your reach beyond YouTube's borders.
3. TikTok: As one of the fastest-growing social media platforms, TikTok offers a unique opportunity to create short, engaging videos that can go viral. Consider repurposing your YouTube content or creating exclusive content for TikTok to tap into its massive user base.
4. Instagram: While primarily a photo-sharing platform, Instagram's IGTV feature allows you to upload longer videos. Leverage your existing Instagram following to promote your YouTube channel and drive traffic to your content.

Remember to tailor your content to each platform's audience and format. Experiment with different types of content and engage with the community to maximize your reach.

10.4.3 Exploring Live Streaming and Podcasting

Live streaming and podcasting are two powerful mediums that can help you expand your brand and connect with your audience on a deeper level. Here's how you can utilize these platforms:

1. Live streaming: Platforms like Twitch, Facebook Live, and YouTube Live allow you to interact with your audience in real-time. Consider hosting live Q&A sessions, behind-the-scenes streams, or even gaming sessions to engage with your viewers on a more personal level.
2. Podcasting: Podcasts have gained immense popularity in recent years, offering a unique way to share your expertise and connect with your audience. Consider starting a podcast where you discuss topics related to your YouTube channel or invite guests to share their insights.

Promote your live streams and podcast episodes on your YouTube channel and social media platforms to attract your existing audience and reach new listeners.

10.4.4 Expanding Your Brand Beyond YouTube

Expanding your brand beyond YouTube involves exploring various platforms and mediums to reach a wider audience. Here are a few additional strategies to consider:

1. Social media presence: Maintain an active presence on social media platforms such as Twitter, Facebook, and Instagram. Engage with your audience, share updates, and promote your content to attract new viewers.
2. Guest appearances: Collaborate with other content creators, industry experts, or influencers by appearing on their channels or podcasts.

This cross-promotion can help you tap into their audience and gain exposure to new viewers.

3. Public speaking and events: Consider participating in industry conferences, panels, or workshops related to your niche. This not only establishes you as an authority in your field but also allows you to network with like-minded individuals and potential collaborators.

4. Merchandise and branding: Create merchandise such as t-shirts, hats, or stickers featuring your channel's branding. This not only helps you monetize your brand but also serves as a form of promotion when your viewers wear or use your merchandise.

Remember, expanding your brand beyond YouTube requires consistency, dedication, and a willingness to explore new opportunities. By utilizing different platforms and mediums, you can reach a wider audience and establish yourself as a prominent figure in your niche.

11 Measuring Success and Setting Future Goals

11.1 Tracking Your Channel's Growth and Performance

Once you have started your journey as a YouTube creator, it is essential to track the growth and performance of your channel. Tracking your channel's progress will help you understand what is working well and what areas need improvement. By analyzing the data and metrics provided by YouTube Analytics, you can make informed decisions to optimize your content and strategies. In this section, we will explore the key metrics to track and how to use them effectively.

11.1.1 Understanding YouTube Analytics

YouTube Analytics is a powerful tool provided by the platform that gives you detailed insights into your channel's performance. It provides data on various metrics such as views, watch time, audience demographics, traffic sources, and engagement. To access YouTube Analytics, go to your YouTube Studio dashboard and click on the "Analytics" tab.

Views and Watch Time

Views and watch time are fundamental metrics that indicate how many people are watching your videos and how long they are watching. Views represent the number of times your videos have been watched, while watch time measures the total amount of time viewers have spent watching your content. These metrics are crucial for understanding the overall popularity and engagement of your channel.

Audience Demographics

Understanding your audience demographics is essential for creating content that resonates with your target viewers. YouTube Analytics provides data on the age, gender, and geographic location of your audience. By analyzing this information, you can tailor your content to better meet the preferences and interests of your viewers.

Traffic Sources

YouTube Analytics also provides insights into where your viewers are coming from. It shows the different sources that drive traffic to your channel, such as YouTube search, suggested videos, external websites, and social media platforms. By identifying the most significant traffic sources, you can optimize your promotional strategies and focus on channels that bring in the most engaged viewers.

Engagement Metrics

Engagement metrics measure how viewers interact with your content. These include metrics such as likes, dislikes, comments, shares, and subscribers gained or lost. Monitoring these metrics allows you to gauge the level of audience engagement and identify which videos are resonating the most with your viewers. Additionally, paying attention to comments and feedback can provide valuable insights for improving your content and building a loyal community.

11.1.2 Setting Goals and Key Performance Indicators (KPIs)

To effectively track your channel's growth and performance, it is crucial to set specific goals and key performance indicators (KPIs). Goals provide a clear direction for your channel, while KPIs help you measure progress towards those goals. Here are some examples of goals and corresponding KPIs:

Goal: Increase Views and Watch Time

- KPI: Total views and watch time
- KPI: Average view duration
- KPI: Audience retention rate

By setting goals related to views and watch time, you can focus on creating engaging content that keeps viewers hooked and encourages them to watch more of your videos.

Goal: Expand Audience Reach

- KPI: Subscribers gained
- KPI: Increase in audience demographics (age, gender, location)
- KPI: Growth in traffic sources

Expanding your audience reach is crucial for building a loyal fan base. By setting goals related to audience growth, you can track your progress in attracting new viewers and expanding your channel's reach.

Goal: Enhance Audience Engagement

- KPI: Likes, dislikes, and comments
- KPI: Shares and social media mentions
- KPI: Increase in engagement rate

Audience engagement is a key indicator of the success of your content. By setting goals related to engagement, you can focus on creating videos that resonate with your viewers and encourage them to interact with your content.

11.1.3 Analyzing and Utilizing YouTube Analytics

Once you have set your goals and identified the relevant KPIs, it's time to analyze the data provided by YouTube Analytics and use it to optimize your channel's performance. Here are some tips for effectively analyzing and utilizing YouTube Analytics:

Regularly Review Your Metrics

Make it a habit to regularly review your channel's metrics. Set aside dedicated time each week or month to analyze the data and track your progress towards your goals. By consistently monitoring your metrics, you can identify trends, patterns, and areas that need improvement.

Identify Successful Videos

Analyze the performance of your individual videos to identify which ones are resonating the most with your audience. Look for videos with high view counts, watch time, and engagement metrics. By understanding what makes these videos successful, you can replicate those elements in future content.

Experiment and Iterate

YouTube Analytics provides valuable insights, but it's essential to experiment and iterate based on the data. Test different video formats, topics, and promotional strategies to see what works best for your channel. Use the data from YouTube Analytics to make data-driven decisions and continuously improve your content and strategies.

Adjust Your Strategies

If you notice that certain videos or strategies are not performing as expected, don't be afraid to make adjustments. Use the insights from YouTube Analytics to identify areas that need improvement and develop new strategies to address them. Flexibility and adaptability are key to long-term success on YouTube.

Tracking your channel's growth and performance is an ongoing process. By regularly reviewing your metrics, setting goals, and utilizing YouTube Analytics effectively, you can make informed decisions to optimize your content, engage your audience, and achieve long-term success as a YouTube creator.

11.2 Setting Realistic Milestones and Targets

Setting realistic milestones and targets is crucial for measuring your progress and staying motivated on your journey to becoming a viral YouTube video creator. In this section, we will discuss the importance of setting milestones, how to define them, and how to track your progress effectively.

Why Setting Milestones is Important

Setting milestones provides you with a clear roadmap and helps you break down your ultimate goal of becoming a viral YouTube video creator into smaller, achievable targets. These milestones act as checkpoints along your journey, allowing you to track your progress and make adjustments to your strategies if needed. They also provide a sense of accomplishment and motivation as you reach each milestone, keeping you focused and determined.

Defining Your Milestones

When defining your milestones, it's important to consider both short-term and long-term goals. Short-term milestones are smaller targets that you can achieve within a few days or weeks, while long-term milestones are larger goals that may take several months to accomplish. Here are some examples of milestones you can set:

Short-Term Milestones

1. Increase your subscriber count by a certain number within a week.
2. Improve your video editing skills by learning a new technique or software.
3. Increase your video views by a specific percentage within a month.
4. Collaborate with another YouTuber in your niche within two weeks.
5. Receive a certain number of likes and comments on your videos within a week.

Long-Term Milestones

1. Reach a specific number of subscribers within six months.
2. Generate a consistent monthly income from your YouTube channel within a year.
3. Have one of your videos go viral and reach a million views within a year.
4. Establish partnerships with brands and sponsors within a year.
5. Become recognized as an authority in your niche within two years.

Tracking Your Progress

Once you have defined your milestones, it's important to track your progress to ensure you are on the right path. Here are some effective ways to track your progress:

Analytics and Metrics

Utilize YouTube's analytics tools to monitor your channel's growth, including metrics such as subscriber count, video views, watch time, and engagement. Regularly review these metrics to identify trends and areas for improvement. Set specific targets for each metric and track your progress towards achieving them.

Goal Tracking Spreadsheet

Create a goal tracking spreadsheet where you can record your milestones, target dates, and actual achievements. This spreadsheet will serve as a visual representation of your progress and help you stay organized. Update it regularly to keep track of your milestones and adjust your strategies if necessary.

Regular Evaluations

Schedule regular evaluations of your channel's performance and progress. This can be done on a monthly or quarterly basis. During these evaluations, analyze your achievements, identify areas for improvement, and adjust your strategies accordingly. Celebrate your successes and learn from any setbacks or challenges you may have faced.

Adjusting Your Strategies

As you track your progress and evaluate your performance, you may need to adjust your strategies to stay on track towards your milestones. Here are some tips for adjusting your strategies effectively:

Identify What's Working and What's Not

Analyze the strategies and techniques that have been successful in helping you achieve your milestones. Identify the factors that contributed to their success and consider replicating them in future videos. Similarly, identify any strategies that have not yielded the desired results and make necessary adjustments or abandon them altogether.

Stay Up-to-Date with Trends and Algorithm Changes

YouTube's algorithm and viewer preferences are constantly evolving. Stay informed about the latest trends, algorithm changes, and viewer preferences in your niche. Adapt your content and strategies accordingly to ensure you stay relevant and continue to attract and engage your audience.

Seek Feedback and Learn from Others

Engage with your audience and seek feedback on your videos. Pay attention to constructive criticism and use it to improve your content and strategies. Additionally, learn from successful YouTubers in your niche by studying their techniques, analyzing their content, and implementing similar strategies in your own unique way.

Conclusion

Setting realistic milestones and targets is essential for measuring your progress and staying motivated on your journey to becoming a viral YouTube video creator. By defining your milestones, tracking your progress, and adjusting your strategies, you can effectively work towards achieving your goals. Remember to celebrate your achievements along the way and stay committed to continuous improvement.

11.3 Evaluating and Adjusting Your Strategies

Once you have implemented your strategies and started to see some growth and success on your YouTube channel, it is important to regularly evaluate and adjust your strategies to ensure continued progress. Evaluating your strategies allows you to identify what is working well and what may need improvement, while adjusting your strategies helps you stay relevant and adapt to changes in the YouTube platform and audience preferences. In this section, we will discuss the key steps to effectively evaluate and adjust your strategies for long-term success on YouTube.

11.3.1 Analyzing Your Channel's Performance

The first step in evaluating your strategies is to analyze your channel's performance. YouTube provides a wealth of analytics and data that can help you understand how your videos are performing and how your audience is engaging with your content. Some key metrics to consider when analyzing your channel's performance include:

- **Views and watch time:** Monitor the number of views your videos are receiving and the amount of time viewers are spending watching your content. This will give you an idea of how engaging your videos are and whether viewers are watching them in their entirety.
- **Audience retention:** Pay attention to the audience retention graph in your YouTube analytics, which shows you the percentage of viewers who continue watching your video at each moment. This will help you identify any drop-off points in your videos and make adjustments to keep viewers engaged.
- **Engagement metrics:** Look at metrics such as likes, dislikes, comments, and shares to gauge how well your audience is engaging with your content. High engagement indicates that your videos are resonating with your viewers and generating interest.

- **Demographics:** Understand the demographics of your audience, including their age, gender, and location. This information can help you tailor your content to better meet the preferences and interests of your target audience.

By regularly monitoring these metrics and analyzing your channel's performance, you can gain valuable insights into what is working well and what areas may need improvement.

11.3.2 Gathering Feedback from Your Audience

In addition to analyzing your channel's performance through analytics, it is also important to gather feedback directly from your audience. Your viewers are a valuable source of information and can provide insights into what they enjoy about your content and what they would like to see more of. Here are some ways to gather feedback from your audience:

- **Comments:** Encourage your viewers to leave comments on your videos and actively respond to them. This will not only help you understand their thoughts and opinions but also foster a sense of community and engagement on your channel.
- **Surveys and polls:** Create surveys or polls using platforms like Google Forms or YouTube's Community tab to gather feedback on specific topics or ideas. This can help you understand your audience's preferences and make informed decisions about your content.
- **Social media engagement:** Engage with your audience on social media platforms like Twitter, Instagram, or Facebook. Ask questions, respond to comments, and participate in conversations to gain insights into what your audience is interested in.

By actively seeking feedback from your audience, you can gain a deeper understanding of their preferences and make adjustments to your content and strategies accordingly.

11.3.3 Experimenting with New Ideas

To keep your channel fresh and engaging, it is important to continuously experiment with new ideas and content formats. This can help you attract new viewers, retain existing ones, and stay ahead of the competition. Here are some ways to experiment with new ideas:

- **Try different video formats:** Explore different video formats such as tutorials, vlogs, challenges, or interviews to see what resonates best with your audience. Pay attention to the performance of each format and adjust your content strategy accordingly.
- **Collaborate with other creators:** Collaborating with other YouTubers can introduce your channel to new audiences and bring fresh perspectives to your content. Experiment with collaborations and assess their impact on your channel's growth and engagement.
- **Introduce new segments or series:** Consider introducing new segments or series on your channel to provide variety and keep your audience engaged. This could include Q&A sessions, behind-the-scenes footage, or special themed videos.

By experimenting with new ideas, you can discover what works best for your channel and continuously evolve your content to meet the changing needs and preferences of your audience.

11.3.4 Staying Updated with YouTube Trends and Algorithm Changes

YouTube is constantly evolving, and staying updated with the latest trends and algorithm changes is crucial for long-term success. The YouTube algorithm determines which videos are recommended to viewers, so understanding how it works can help you optimize your content for maximum visibility. Here are some ways to stay updated:

- **Follow YouTube's Creator Insider channel:** YouTube's Creator Insider channel provides updates on algorithm changes, new features, and best practices. Subscribe to this channel to stay informed about the latest developments.

- **Stay connected with the YouTube community:** Engage with other creators, join forums, and participate in discussions to stay updated with the latest trends and strategies in the YouTube community.
- **Attend conferences and workshops:** Attend YouTube conferences, workshops, and webinars to learn from industry experts and gain insights into the latest trends and strategies.

By staying updated with YouTube trends and algorithm changes, you can make informed decisions about your content and strategies, ensuring that you remain relevant and visible to your target audience.

11.3.5 Setting New Goals and Milestones

As you evaluate and adjust your strategies, it is important to set new goals and milestones to keep yourself motivated and focused. Setting realistic and achievable goals will help you measure your progress and track your success. Here are some tips for setting new goals:

- **Be specific:** Clearly define what you want to achieve and set specific targets. For example, aim to increase your subscriber count by a certain percentage or reach a specific number of views on a particular video.
- **Break it down:** Break your goals into smaller, manageable milestones. This will make them more attainable and allow you to track your progress more effectively.
- **Regularly review and adjust:** Regularly review your goals and adjust them as needed. As you gain more insights and data, you may need to revise your goals to align with your channel's growth and performance.

By setting new goals and milestones, you can stay motivated and continue to strive for success on your YouTube journey.

In conclusion, evaluating and adjusting your strategies is a crucial step in achieving long-term success on YouTube. By analyzing your channel's performance, gathering feedback from your audience, experimenting with new ideas, staying updated with YouTube trends, and setting new goals, you can ensure that your channel continues to grow and thrive. Remember, success on YouTube is a continuous process, and by consistently evaluating and adjusting your strategies, you can stay ahead of the curve and become a true YouTube sensation.

11.4 Planning for Long-Term Success

Congratulations! You have successfully embarked on your journey to becoming a YouTube sensation. By now, you have learned the ins and outs of the YouTube platform, developed engaging content, built an audience, optimized your channel, monetized your videos, engaged with your viewers, promoted your videos, collaborated with other YouTubers, overcome challenges, expanded your YouTube presence, and measured your success. Now, it's time to plan for long-term success and set goals that will propel you even further in your YouTube career.

11.4.1 Reflecting on Your Journey

Before diving into planning for the future, take a moment to reflect on your journey so far. Consider the milestones you have achieved, the challenges you have overcome, and the lessons you have learned. Reflecting on your past experiences will provide valuable insights that will guide you in setting realistic and achievable goals for the future.

11.4.2 Defining Your Long-Term Vision

To plan for long-term success, it is crucial to have a clear vision of where you want to be in the future. Take some time to envision your ultimate goals as a YouTube creator. What kind of content do you want to create? How big of an audience do you want to reach? Do you want to become a recognized influencer in your niche? Defining your long-term vision will serve as a guiding light as you set your goals and make strategic decisions.

11.4.3 Setting SMART Goals

Now that you have a clear vision, it's time to set SMART goals that will help you achieve it. SMART stands for Specific, Measurable, Achievable, Relevant, and Time-bound. Let's break down each component:

1. Specific: Your goals should be clear and well-defined. Instead of saying, "I want more subscribers," specify the number of subscribers you want to reach within a specific timeframe.
2. Measurable: Your goals should be quantifiable so that you can track your progress. For example, instead of saying, "I want to increase my video views," specify the percentage increase you want to achieve.
3. Achievable: Your goals should be realistic and attainable. Consider your current resources, capabilities, and constraints. Setting goals that are too far-fetched may lead to frustration and disappointment.
4. Relevant: Your goals should align with your long-term vision and be relevant to your YouTube channel. Ensure that each goal contributes to your overall growth and success.
5. Time-bound: Your goals should have a specific timeframe for completion. This adds a sense of urgency and helps you stay focused and motivated. Set deadlines for each goal to keep yourself accountable.

11.4.4 Prioritizing Your Goals

With your SMART goals in place, it's time to prioritize them based on their importance and impact. Not all goals are created equal, and some may have a more significant influence on your long-term success than others. Consider the goals that will have the most significant impact on your channel's growth and prioritize them accordingly. This will help you allocate your time, resources, and efforts effectively.

11.4.5 Breaking Down Your Goals into Actionable Steps

Once you have prioritized your goals, break them down into smaller, actionable steps. This will make them more manageable and less overwhelming. Each step should be specific, measurable, and time-bound. Create a timeline or a roadmap that outlines the sequence of steps you need to take to achieve each goal. This will provide you with a clear path to follow and keep you on track.

11.4.6 Seeking Continuous Learning and Improvement

To ensure long-term success on YouTube, it's essential to embrace a mindset of continuous learning and improvement. The digital landscape is constantly evolving, and new trends, strategies, and techniques emerge regularly. Stay updated with the latest industry news, attend conferences or webinars, and engage with other creators to learn from their experiences. Continuously refine your content creation process, optimize your channel, and adapt to changes in the YouTube algorithm.

11.4.7 Building a Supportive Network

Surround yourself with a supportive network of fellow creators, mentors, and industry professionals. Collaborate with other YouTubers, join online communities and forums, and attend networking events. Building relationships with like-minded individuals will not only provide you with valuable insights and advice but also open doors to new opportunities and collaborations.

11.4.8 Tracking and Evaluating Your Progress

Regularly track and evaluate your progress towards your goals. Use YouTube Analytics to monitor your channel's growth, engagement metrics, and audience demographics. Analyze the performance of your videos, identify patterns, and adjust your strategies accordingly. Celebrate your achievements along the way and learn from any setbacks or challenges you encounter.

11.4.9 Staying Consistent and Persistent

Consistency and persistence are key to long-term success on YouTube. Stay committed to your content creation schedule, engage with your audience regularly, and consistently deliver high-quality videos. Building a loyal audience takes time, so don't get discouraged if you don't see immediate results. Stay persistent, learn from your experiences, and keep pushing forward.

11.4.10 Celebrating Milestones and Setting New Goals

As you achieve your goals and reach significant milestones, take the time to celebrate your accomplishments. Recognize the hard work and dedication that went into your success. Once you have celebrated, set new goals that will challenge you and push you further. Remember, success is a journey, and there is always room for growth and improvement.

By planning for long-term success, setting SMART goals, and staying committed to continuous learning and improvement, you are well on your way to becoming a YouTube sensation. Embrace the challenges, celebrate the victories, and enjoy the incredible journey that awaits you. Good luck!